Nonya Heritage Kitchen

Text copyright © 2016 Ong Jin Teong
Food photography copyright © 2016 Ee Kay Gie
Photographs on pages 4, 6, 8, 12, 62/63, 198/199 and 266
    are from the author's family collection

Published by
Landmark Books Pte Ltd
5001 Beach Road,
02-73/74
Singapore 199588

Landmark Books is an imprint of
Landmark Books Pte Ltd

ISBN 978-981-4189-68-2

Printed in Singapore

NONYA HERITAGE KITCHEN

Origins, Utensils and Recipes

ONG JIN TEONG

·LANDMARK·BOOKS·

CONTENTS

JEE CHIM WITH MY DAUGHTER, KIM.

PREFACE

Mdm Lim Say Choo, my wife's *jee chim* or second aunt, was my mentor for making Nonya *kuih*s.

As their son was young when her husband passed away, *jee chim* resorted to making and selling *kuih*s to support her family. She made a large assortment of *kuih*s for festivals and weddings, over 120 pieces of each type per assignment. It was hard work.

Jee chim did not write down her recipes and was used to cooking large quantities. So, my wife and I prepared large amounts in our masterclasses, much to the delight of our friends and family who got their share of the food.

Jee chim's instinctive method of cooking made the process of recording and fine-tuning recipes a long and challenging one. First, I made a tentative list of ingredients and she would say that she doesn't use a particular ingredient or added others. Then she would give an idea of the quantities required, measured by bowls or in handfuls. At the masterclasses, she told me what to do and I followed her instructions. Ever so often, she explained some of the finer points of wrapping or moulding a *kuih*. I weighed and recorded all the ingredients used. Liquids were a challenge because she just poured them in without measurement.

The next stage was to go through my scanty notes (it is not easy to cook and make notes) and write a draft. Then there were telephone conversations or a visit for clarification.

Once the first draft recipe was completed, I prepared the *kuih* on my own. If it did not taste right or have the correct texture, it was back to *jee chim* for further advice. Often, it took more than one iteration to get the taste and consistency of the *kuih* of my youth.

Sadly, *jee chim* passed away in 2014, and I gratefully dedicate this book to her memory.

Ong Jin Teong
2016

INTRODUCTION

The early Chinese seafarers of Fujian province ventured south along the China coast to reach Vietnam and Thailand, and further south to Indonesia and the Malay Peninsula. This Chinese maritime trade with Southeast Asia peaked during the Yuan dynasty (1279-1378). During the later Ming (1378-1644) and Qing (1644-1911) dynasties, overseas trade was banned in China, resulting in the permanent settlement of the Chinese in Southeast Asia. And, as these traders were unaccompanied by womenfolk, many married the local women and started families.

This fusion of the Chinese and the local Malay cultures resulted in what we know as the Nonya/Baba or Peranakan culture where the men are known as Babas and the ladies, Nonyas. In old Malaya, the early Peranakan community sprung up in Malacca which had been colonised in turn by the Portuguese, Dutch and English since the 16th century. When Penang was founded by the English East India Company in 1786, a Peranakan community was established in Georgetown by Chinese settlers who came from Kedah and Southern Thailand. A similar community was established in Singapore when Raffles arrived in 1819 and the already-established Peranakan families from Malacca, Penang and the Indonesian Riau Islands moved to the new settlement because of the prospects of trade.

Hence, the Nonyas and Babas of Malaya were predominantly centred in what was known as the British Straits Settlements made up of Singapore, Malacca and Penang. This is why the Peranakans are also known as the Straits Chinese.

While the Babas and Nonyas kept their Chinese traditions, rituals and beliefs, they adopted many Malay customs and superstitions. This intermarriage of cultures gave rise

A TRADITIONAL NONYA KITCHEN MODERNISED WITH CERAMIC TILES.

to a new culture – and cuisine.

A number of factors could have contributed to the evolution of Nonya food. The first local women to marry Chinese settlers probably wished to please the palates of their husbands with the food the men loved. They embraced the festive dishes of south China and ensured that food prepared during festivals of their own culture was introduced to their households. They modified Chinese food by substituting and including Southeast Asian ingredients. Dishes brought in by the colonial community inspired them. The cooking utensils of Malay, Chinese and European heritage shaped particular dishes. And, like cooks of every era, they shared recipes with each other, thereby establishing popular dishes that would define their cuisine.

Thus, Nonya cuisine is an early example of fusion food, one that evolved from this integration of Malay and Hokkien food with the colonial cuisines of Portugal, the Netherlands and England.

Malay dishes are characterized by the use of coconut milk, sour tamarind, piquant shallots and garlic, aromatic lemongrass, and fragrant gingers like turmeric, galangal and lesser galangal. Root vegetables like tapioca, sweet potato and yam are also commonly used. The many leaves and shoots used for flavouring in the Malay kitchen include kaffir lime leaves, a variety of wild pepper leaf known as *daun kadok*, pandan and Polygonum. Jade-green pandan is also used for colouring, as are *bunga telang* – the blue Butterfly Pea flower, and bright orange turmeric. *Belacan*, the pungent dried shrimp paste, is another very important Malay ingredient. Chillies, so essential to Malay cuisine, were introduced to the region by Portuguese colonizers. Nonya dishes like Roti Jala, Acar Awak, and Sesargon arc predominantly Malay, their key ingredients being spices and coconut that are common in every kampong.

The food products from Fujian province shaped Hokkien cuisine: Seafood from the coastal waters, and bamboo shoots, fungi, fruits and nuts from the mountainous forests. So, Hokkien influence in Nonya cuisine can be clearly seen in the use of ingredients like crab, pickled vegetable, bamboo shoots and beans. These are the main ingredients of classic Nonya dishes like Bak Wan Kepiting, Kiam Chai Ark, Koay Pai Ti and Ang Koo Kuih.

Rice, cultivated both in China and Southeast Asia, brought Malay and Hokkien food together in Nonya cuisine in its various whole and ground forms. Thus, we have, Nasi Kunyit and Ketupat from Malay cuisine, Bak Chang and Kuih Ee from the Chinese, and Kuih Koci and Ondeh Ondeh that can be traced to both cultures.

A large number of recipes in this book are for snacks prepared for festive occasions celebrated by the Chinese, Malays and Peranakans. Most of these Nonya *kuih*s have either Malay or Hokkien origins, and it is no coincidence that the words in Hokkien, Malay and Indonesian for them are *koay*, *kuih* and *kue*. The origin is the Chinese character 粿, which is a combination of the characters for 'rice' and 'fruit'. Some others, like Sugee Cake and Kuih Kapit are from the culinary traditions of the European colonials.

Boiled, steamed, fried, grilled or baked, *kuih*s are mainly sweet but some are savoury; even the sweet ones have a touch of saltiness, especially if fresh grated coconut or coconut milk is one of the ingredients. Hence, there is a great variety of *kuih*s which could be variously described as cakes, pastries, biscuits, dumplings, fritters and cookies which come in different shapes, sizes, flavours, textures and colours. Chang or rice dumplings, Otak Otak and Kuih Koci Santan are are wrapped with leaves into a pyramid shape. Kuih Koci and Abok Abok are wrapped into cones and Kueh Ee and Ondeh Ondeh are formed into balls.

The Penang Nonyas are more particular about shapes and sizes of their *kuih*s, and those served at wedding receptions were smaller, more *chomel*, the Malay word for 'dainty and pretty'. In Penang, Kuih Talam, Kuih Lapis (Kau Chan Kuih), Huat Kuih, and Coconut Candy are cut into diamonds while Kuih Bengka Ubi Kayu and Pulut Taitai are traditionally sliced into rectangles.

In the preparation of their food, the Nonyas use a large variety of utensils which originate from all over the world, particularly China and India. You could say that these utensils have shaped Nonya cuisine literally and metaphorically.

The grinding stone (*batu giling*) and the mortar and pestle (*lesong*) are commonly used for grinding and pounding spices. Both are very ancient utensils. The *batu giling* is most probably is of Indian origin, although something similar had been used in South America to grind corn for ages. Similarly, the mortar and pestle had also been used by the Mayans and Aztecs for more than six centuries. The Nonya equivalent, or *lesong*, are made of granite, but other versions made of wood, marble, ceramics and even glass are in use in Southeast Asian and other parts of the world.

Ground rice is widely used by the Nonyas for preparing their *kuih*s. In the days before rice flour was readily available in shops, raw rice was ground using a stone mill (*cheok bo*), another ancient utensil found in China and India.

Besides the edible parts of the coconut, virtually every portion of the coconut tree has some use in the Nonya kitchen. Coconut shells are still being made into ladles called *senduk* in Malay, and the leaves into baskets and used for wrapping food. Not many today know that Satay sticks were traditionally made of *lidi*s, the the midribs of coconut leaflets.

The moulds and pans which Nonyas use for preparing their *kuih*s likewise reflect the diverse culinary influences of Peranakan cuisine. Wooden moulds, such as the intricately carved ones used for Ang Koo and Kuih Bangkit come from Chinese culture. The claypots or *blangah* hark back to those used in India. The clippers for making Kuih Kapit or

Love Letters are by intent and purposes identical to the Dutch Knieperties waffle irons. Likewise, the Kuih Bahulu pan could have a Portuguese origin although the Chinese have similar sponge cakes. The mould for making Koay Pai Ti shells and the origin of the dish is less clear; the names Singapore Poh Piah and Syonanto Pie point to Singapore while Java Kwei Patti and Kroket Tjanker suggest Java and Dutch Indonesia.

On the other hand, the Roti Jala spout is an entirely Nonya invention. A clever nonya, frustrated from drizzling batter from her fingers to make the lacy pancake, probably commissioned her local metalsmith to make her an inovative cup with many thin spouts.

All these utensils and ingredients enabled the Nonyas of old to create their culinary wonders, often without recorded recipes but with the instinctive estimation of quantities that characterize cooking expertise and cooking with love.

So, it was that in traditional Peranakan households, girls were trained from a young age to cook, starting with menial tasks like plucking the roots off beansprouts, peeling onions or shelling prawns, graduating to the rythmic use of the mortar and pestle and then to the frying of a perfect spice paste, and finally, mastery of staple and festive dishes. Indeed, maidens without culinary skills once found it difficult to find a husband. It therefore needs to be recognised that it was this Asian and particularly Chinese out-moded attitude of women being bound to home and kitchen that helped develop and establish Nonya cuisine.

LADIES FROM THE AUTHOR'S FAMILY MAKING CURRY PUFFS.

Weights & Measures

The Babas and Nonyas do not traditionally use definitive measures. It is all done by rough estimation or what is known as *agak agak* in both Baba Malay and Malay. I looked up the phrase in a Malay dictionary and it means "most probably, maybe, fairly", underlining the measurement uncertainties! The Nonyas also used a handful of this and a bowl of that in their recipes. It is all done by taste, feel and experience. I also cook like that if I am not recording a recipe. A handful or a fistful of ingredient is *mek* in Penang Hokkien, and since a Baba's (male) *mek* would be bigger than a (female) Nonya's, it adds more uncertainties to Nonya cooking.

I have been through many older recipes and, in terms of weights and measures, a large variety of units were used. Many early recipes, including some of my mother's, use the cost of the ingredients – 10 cents of dried chillies, 15 cents of shallots or 5 cents of *belacan*. I found a version of her Otak Otak recipe with the quantity of many ingredients given in cents. It would be interesting to use these recipes according to original costs but generally scaled up to take into account inflation. We would certainly end up with a different retro dish since inflation is so different for each of the various ingredients. It would be an interesting project indeed!

In compiling my recipes, I try to find a convenient unit for measuring small quantities of ingredients like ground spices. The teaspoon is a convenient measure to use, but what is a suitable unit of smaller quantities are involved? Looking at the Ang Moh Tau Yew (Worcestershire sauce) recipe that my father wrote, because he did not have the miniature Chinese balancing scales known as *chin* or *daching* used by *sinseh* in medical halls, he resorted to counting the number of seed spices required. It is fine counting the number

THE WEIGHT OF A *KATI* IS EQUIVALENT TO A POUND OR 605 GRAMS.

of peppercorns but, when it comes to smaller spices like fennel and cumin, it becomes rather tricky counting 250 grains!

Chupak and Gantang

Many old recipes use *chupak* and *gantang* as measures for the amount of rice or grains. We used to buy rice from the *chai tiama* or local provision shop. That is where we bought most of our provisions and household products before supermarkets appeared. *Chupak* and *gantang* are volumetric measures. Rice is poured into a *chupak* or *gantang* container and a wooden stick like a ruler is used to level the rice which is then poured into a paper bag made of old newspaper. We were all very green in those day; old newspapers were recycled. These were not local newspapers but foreign ones since the local newspaper circulation in the past was rather low. We learned in schools, then, that four *chupak*s makes a *gantang* and two pints make a quart and four quarts makes a gallon. I was trying to figure out the size of the *chupak* and *gantang* container when I realised that one *chupak* is equivalent to a quart or two pints and one *gantang* is a gallon.

A *gantang* is commonly used as a dry volumetric measure in Southeast Asia, and a weight measure in some parts of the region. The British standardized it to an imperial gallon (4.54 litres) in the countries under their influence. In Indonesia, it is approximately 8.6 litres but was 8.4 litres when it was under Dutch rule. Thus, the *gantang* capacity does not appear to have been standardized.

There are several references which suggest that a *chupak* has the capacity of half a coconut shell, but we don't know the size of the coconut! In Malaya, a *chupak* of rice weighs about 34 oz or 965 g, approximately one kilogram.

Cigarette Tins, Rice Bowls, Cups and other Measures

In the 1950s, cigarettes were sold in cardboard packs of ten, in flat metal boxes of 20 and in cylindrical tins of fifty cigarettes. Those were the days before filters, hence the height of the tins was the length of a cigarette without the filter. For a very long time, the cigarette tin was used daily in most households to measure rice. I have a friend who still uses the cigarette tin that was used by her mother-in-law for that purpose. A cigarette tin was also used as a convenient measure of dried ingredients like flour and sugar. Old cookery

THE *GANTANG* IS ALSO USED DURING THE NONYA 12-DAY WEDDING CEREMONY. DURING THE HAIR-COMBING RITUAL, THE BRIDEGROOM SITS ON THE *GANTANG* RICE BUCKET WITH THE OPENING FACING DOWNWARDS, WHILE THE BRIDE SITS ON THE OPEN *GANTANG*. IT IS NOT COMFORTABLE AND THE IMPLICATION IS THAT MARRIED LIFE IS NOT EASY.

books, even those published in the Sixties, gave handy measures of a cigarette tin for common ingredients like rice and flour.

According to one cookbook, a tin filled to half inch from the top contains 4 oz of unsifted flour. It is different if the flour has been sifted. In my aunt Khoo Paik Choo's book, *Malaysian Cookery for Schools*, she listed the weights of one level cigarette tin of food like rice (6 oz, 170 g), sultanas or currants (5 oz, 142 g) and beans (7 oz, 198 g). For liquid measure, the old cigarette tins have a capacity of about half an imperial pint (260 ml).

This traditional practice of using a cigarette tin as a measure for dry ingredients was also prevalent in India, Sri Lanka, East and North Africa and the Middle East.

When I asked my cousin Sandy about her recipes, she would estimate some of her ingredients in terms of a Chinese rice bowl which has a diameter of 11-cm at the rim and a height of 5 cm. My *jee chim*, Mdm Lim Say Choo, who is the second aunt on my wife's side of the family, also uses the bowl as a measure of her ingredients. I had to ask for a sample bowl to find out the capacity.

I checked the capacity of various rice bowls (trust an engineer like me to do that!) and found that it could vary between 270 and 300 ml even for bowls of the same design. I realized only recently that in using bowls as measures, some Nonyas don't fill them to the brim. This makes following old Nonya recipes so much more challenging!

Cups were also used as a measure for ingredients, especially for cake and desserts. My understanding is that a British or Imperial cup refers to a breakfast cup which has a capacity of 10 fluid ounces (284 ml) or half an imperial pint. The teacup is smaller, with a capacity of one third of a pint. The English coffee cups are even smaller. American cups have a capacity of US 8 fluid ounces (about 237 ml) while the US Food and Drug Administration's cup for nutritional and food products is 240 ml. To add to these variations, an Australian standard cup has a capacity of 250 ml. So I shall not to use cups as a measure in this book. Coincidentally, after measuring the capacities of several Chinese rice bowls, I realized that a British breakfast cup and a Chinese rice bowl have virtually the same capacity.

Once, I asked Sandy about a recipe and she said that I should use a marble-size amount of *belacan*. My aunt Khoo Phaik Choo also used marbles to describe the amount of tamarind in her cookery book. I know what she was talking about because I played with marbles when I was young – not the small glass marbles that we still see today but the bigger opaque ones. When writing about this, I thought to myself: what were the marbles made of? The answer to myself: "They were made of marble, stupid!" The ones we played with were made of white stone; I wonder if they were really marble. In one of my mother's recipes, instead of a marble, a ping pong ball was used to estimate the amount required.

Teaspoon and Tablespoons

For measuring small quantities of ingredients, the teaspoon and the tablespoon are used. There is a more common standard for the capacity of spoons around the world. The British, the Australian, and the FDA tablespoons have the same capacity of 15 ml while the US tablespoon has a slightly smaller capacity of 14.7 ml. The difference is not significant in cooking. However, it is important to note that the Australian tablespoon has a capacity four times that of the teaspoon.

Tea leaves were a rare and expensive commodity when tea-drinking was introduced to England around 1660. When the English East India Company started to import tea directly from China in 1710, the price of tea declined, and thus the size of teaspoons increased. By the 1730s, the teaspoon had increased to a third of a tablespoon. Today, the capacity of a British, Australian and US teaspoon is 5 ml although, strictly speaking, a teaspoon as a unit of culinary measure in the US is still one-third of a tablespoon or 4.92892159375 ml.

The British dessertspoon has a 10-ml capacity. This may be of interest to Malaysians, Singaporeans and Southeast Asians in general, who commonly eat with a dessert fork and dessertspoon in combination instead of fork and knife. We use the tablespoon and table fork for serving. I cannot remember ever using a tablespoon in a Western meal when I was growing up.

All spoon measures are leveled. The spoon is filled with the ingredient and a straight knife edge is run across the top edge of the spoon. A rounded spoon means there is as much ingredient above the edge of the spoon as there is below. A heaped spoon is the amount of ingredient that you can scoop up with a spoon without it falling off!

Weighing Machines

These days, I use a digital weighing scale, but in the old days, even normal scales were not readily available. The *daching* was commonly used for weighing but it was not something that every household would have although it was an essential device in provision stores, in markets, and in Chinese medicine shops. It has traditionally been used to weigh everything from the light weights of ingredients for traditional Chinese medicine, live chicken or fresh cuts of meat, to large bags of rice and even rubber sheets.

This weighing device consists of a long, calibrated wooden beam or rod balanced on a fulcrum which is just a string connected to a small hole drilled through the rod. The smaller balancing scales, with slim rods, are held by this string using one hand. For weighing heavy weights, this string, attached to a pole, is replaced by a rope connected to a rafter on the ceiling. On one side of the fulcrum is a standard counter weight, and on the other is the pointer/pivot arrangement which indicates when the scale is balanced. The object to be weighed is placed on a pan or a hook attached to the pointer/pivot. The counter weight is moved along the beam to balance the scale and the weight of the object is read off the calibration on the beam.

The calibrated rods or beams range from about 20 centimetres to over 2 metres; they are made of hardwood. Some of the smaller ones are made of brass or bamboo. The traditional weights read on the calibrated beam are *kati* and *tael*.

The *kati* and *tael* (some old recipes use *tah*) are Chinese measures very commonly used in old Malaya and Singapore. The imperial pound and ounce were introduced when the British spring weighing scales were imported. One *kati* is about 1 pound or about 605 g (normally rounded down to 600 g), and there are 16 *taels* in a *kati*. Counting in binary units seems to be a universal thing because there are 16 ounces to a pound. I have been told that the *daching* used today are calibrated in kilograms.

To ensure that market products were accurately weighed, the Georgetown Municipal Council in Penang provided, in the 1950s, weighing scales to public markets to allow customers to check the weight of the products that they have bought. The scales in those days had both pound and ounces, and *kati* and *tael* calibrations. Even though the counter weights were certified and stamped by the Weights and Measures Authority, customers may still have been short changed because they may not know how to read the weights on the scale.

Most of the counter-weights for *daching*s that I have seen have a register number and the year of issue embossed at the bottom, suggesting that the local Municipal Council then kept a firm control on weighing machines used commercially.

THIS TYPE OF *DACHING* WAS THE COMMON WEIGHING MACHINE USED IN THE MARKETS OF SINGAPORE AND MALAYSIA UP TO THE 1960s.

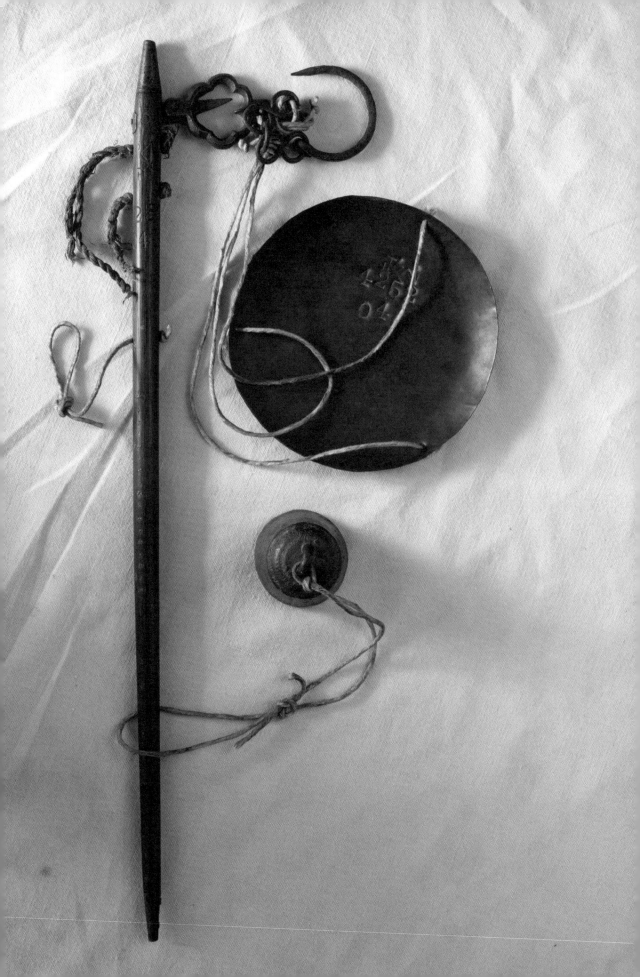

Ginding, Pounding, Slicing

Spices are berries, stems, barks, roots or seeds of tropical shrubs and trees while herbs, some of which could also be considered as spices, are leaves of aromatic plants. They are used to impart flavour, seasoning, aroma, and sometimes colour to food.

Spices, like cinnamon and nutmeg, were already important commodities during the late middle ages. By the 16th century, international relations were influenced by the trade in spices. Nutmeg and pepper were like black gold, similar to what oil is in the 20th and the 21st centuries. Spices became so valuable that, in Europe, financial transactions were carried out in peppercorns.

The quest for spices led to the financing of the voyages of discovery by Christopher Columbus from 1492 by the Spanish, and Vasco de Gama from 1497 by the Portuguese. Their aim was to gain an advantage in the spice trade. At that time, no European had made landfall on the Spice Islands – the source of nutmeg and other spices in the Indonesian archipelago. Columbus could only find chillies, or red peppers, in the New World. Chillies, which are native of Mexico, were later introduced to Southeast Asia by Portuguese navigators in the 16th century, thus changing the diversity of the regional cuisine. Vasco de Gama, after rounding the Cape of Good Hope, reached, in 1498, his objective of Calicut on the Malabar Coast of India – then the major entrepôt of the spice trade. Afonso de Albuquerque further laid the foundation of the eastern Portuguese empire when he established a foothold in Cochin on the western coast of India in 1503.

[LEFT] A SKILLED COOK CAN USE SUCH A CHOPPER TO BOTH CHOP AND SLICE.
[OVERLEAF] A *BATU GILING* IS EFFECTIVE IN GRINDING AND CRUSHING SOFT AND HARD SPICES, SEEDS AND ROOTS.

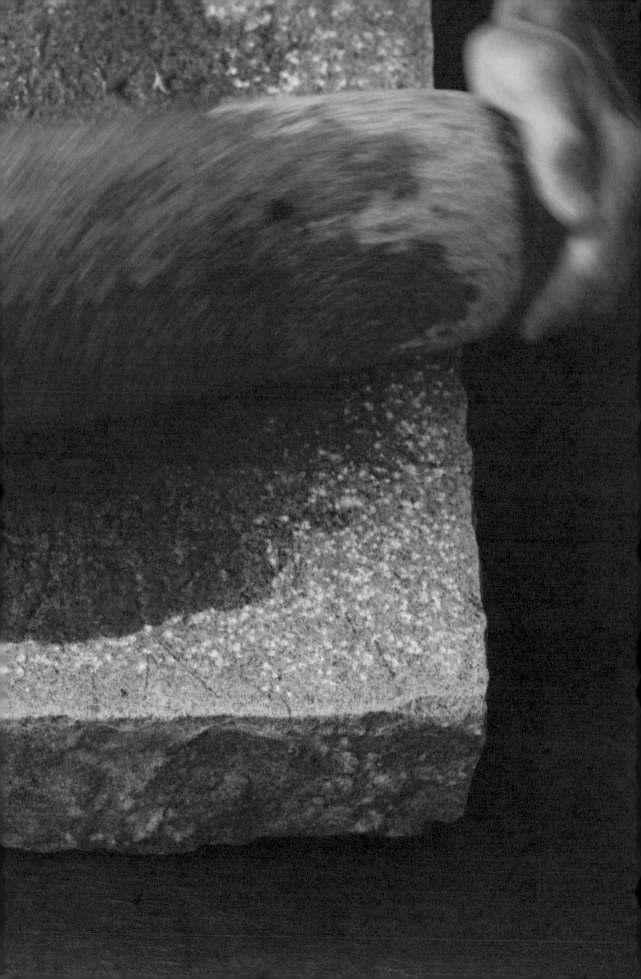

The Spanish redoubled their efforts by financing the first round-the-world trip, circumnavigating westward via the tip of South America, in the hope of finding the Spice Islands. For this, they turned, ironically, to the Portuguese explorer Ferdinand Magellan, who departed Spain for this journey in 1519. Although Magellan was killed in battle in the Philippines during the expedition, his crew and ship did reach Banda in the Spice Islands in 1521. However, de Albuquerque had already taken control of Malacca for the Portuguese in 1511 and had landed in the Spice Islands in 1512.

The Dutch came on the scene in the tail end of the 16th century when their supply of spices were disrupted in Europe. Their first expedition realised a 400 percent profit, which galvanised the Dutch government to form the Dutch East India Company. By the early 20th century, Dutch imperial dominance in Indonesia was complete.

An interesting footnote of the Dutch control of the spice trade is that the Dutch government once dispatched orders to their colonial governors to reduce nutmeg trees and to increase mace trees. They did not know, and many people still do not know today, that both nutmeg and mace are from the fruit of the same tree.

The root spices native to Malaysia, Singapore and the rest of Southeast Asia include shallots and onions, garlic, ginger, turmeric, galangal, and lesser galangal (*cekur*). Ninety-eight percent of Malaysian pepper is grown in Sarawak while nutmeg and cloves are grown in Penang. Cloves are flower buds of the *Syzygium aromaticum* tree and *bunga kantan* is the flower of the torch ginger.

The main herb spices commonly used by Nonyas are Indian curry leaves, laksa leaves (*kesom*), pandan leaves, lemongrass (*serai*), kaffir lime leaves (*limau purut*), and leaves from turmeric (*kunyit*) and lesser galangal (*cekur*) – the latter used mainly in Penang. Wild betel leaves (*daun kadok*) are used more extensively in northern Malaysia, closer to Thailand.

Spices from fruits include tamarind (*assam jawa*), garcinia (*assam gelugor*) and chillies.

Seed spices, most probably brought to Malaya by the early Indian settlers in Kedah, include coriander, fennel, cumin, and cardamom. Most traditional Malay curries do not include these seed spices. Other commonly used spices in Southeast Asia are star anise, candlenut (*buah keras*), and cinnamon.

Rempah is a Malay term used to describe a combination of spices that is traditionally ground together to form a paste using a grinding stone (*batu giling*), or pounded in a mortar and pestle (*lesong*). The main *rempah* ingredients are chillies and shallots. Malays, Nonyas and Eurasians have their own combination of other spices for their *rempah*. The food processor has now replaced the *batu giling* but the granite *lesong* still survives in many Nonya and Malay households.

Belacan, being shrimp paste, is not a spice, but is still an important ingredient in most *rempah* prepared by Nonyas and Malays.

Batu Giling (Grinding Stone)

Although *batu giling* is a Malay name, the tool most probably originated in the Indian sub-continent going back several centuries. *Batu* is 'stone', referring to the granite from which it is made. *Giling* means 'to roll or grind'. There is something similar, called *metate*, used to grind corn in Mexico and other parts of South America.

We have a *batu giling* at home but it is not often used. Even my mother took her *rempah* ingredients across the road to a lady who ground them for her.

The *batu giling* consists of a thick, flat slab of stone and a cylindrical rolling pin made from the same material. The rectangular slab is about 30 cm wide, about 45 cm long and has a thickness of about 10 cm. The rolling pin has a length of about 40 cm, greater than the width of the slab. Called *anak* or 'child' in Malay, it has a diameter of about 10 cm at the centre, tapering slightly toward the ends. The ends of some rolling pins have a knob that fits the hands of the user.

The user sits or stands facing the width of the slab, holding the rolling pin with both hands perpendicular to the length of the slab. The rolling pin is slid forward and back to grind the spices.

With constant use, the surface of the slab, as well as that of the rolling pin, become too smooth, making the grinding less effective. The surfaces therefore have to be reconditioned by making them rough again.

My cousin had a worn *batu giling* and she asked some building workman to roughen the surface with a chisel. Unfortunately, the grooves they made were far too deep. I then volunteered to do something about it. With some difficulty, I got my building contractor to shave off the surface. I think he got it done in a granite workshop. They went on to polish the surface! So we were back to square one! I had to chisel the surface to roughen them – hard labour indeed! I didn't realise till then that granite is such a hard stone.

Cheryll Ng, a friend from the Penang Heritage Food Facebook group, reminded me of the *tukang* ('craftsmen' in Malay) who carried around a stove with burning charcoal.

They repaired leaking pots and pans. Another group of men sharpened knives and scissors, and re-conditioned *batu giling, lesong* and *cheok bo* (rice grinder) as well.

There was also the more specialised *tajam batu* man who worked with a hammer and chisel to make small grooves on the *batu giling*, going in a row from right to left, then left to right and so forth till the surface of the *batu giling* was covered with chisel marks. The same thing was done on the rolling pin. Once this was done, we would take the *batu giling* home and ground some raw rice with it. The rice was then cleaned off with water to complete the reconditioning of the *batu giling*.

You need these small holes or grooves on the *batu giling* for the spices to be effectively ground. These tiny pits trap the *rempah* ingredients and, as the rolling pin moves forward and backward, the bits sticking out of the grooves are ground. Without these grooves, the *rempah* will just be moved from one end of the slab to the other without getting any finer.

There was a *tajam batu* man who went on his bicycle around Macalister Road, near the Pakistani Mosque in Penang. The chisel marks he made were not deep but they were fine and evenly spaced. My classmate, Datuk Oh Chong Peng, who has a lot of experience grinding *rempah* with the *batu giling*, recalled the grooves this man made were very shallow – maybe only 1 mm or so – and cut at a diagonal. I guess each *tukang* has his own way of doing things. Siew Kee, Chong Peng's wife, says that the experts at reconditioning *batu giling* are the tombstone makers.

It is traditional to grind the ingredient whole whether it is ginger, onions or chillies; none of the ingredients are first cut up with a knife. As the ingredients are crushed between the roller and the slab, they break into smaller pieces, after which they are ground by the sliding movement of the roller.

The surface of a well-used *batu giling* will have a slightly concave shape since the middle part of the slab is the most-used surface.

I confess that I have not used a *batu giling* before I started my research into this very ancient device. Now, I find it quite easy to use it for grinding the softer ingredients like onions and chillies. Grinding harder ingredients like lemongrass and galangal is more tedious. However, one bash of the roller on any ingredient will easily break it up.

In Malaya and Singapore, *rempah* sellers in the markets were traditionally Indians. They sold a large variety of *rempah* ground using the *batu giling*. If you tell them what curry you have planned to cook, they will give you the right combination of ground spices, all wrapped up in a banana leaf. In my young days, a packet of *rempah* would cost much less than a dollar, but today the same packet costs several dollars! In the Pulau Tikus market in Penang, a Chinese lady has been selling *rempah* for many years, and plastic bags have replaced her banana leaves.

Lesong (Mortar and Pestle)

Many Malay and Nonya *rempah*s are not meant to be too finely ground, especially if the dry seed spices like coriander, cumin and fennel are not used. A good example is Curry Kapitan, the *rempah* of which should not be too fine to give the curry texture.

To achieve the right texture, the *batu giling* which grinds spices finely is replaced by the *lesong*. A *lesong* is also a better tool for pounding *rempah* if the quantity involved is not large; it is all relative, depending on the size of the pestle and mortar you have. The *lesong* is small enough to be portable compared to the *batu giling* and that is one reason why the *lesong* is still in use today.

For the record, there is also what is called a *lesong kaki* – a large version of the mortar, except that the pestle is connected to a wooden lever that is operated by foot (*kaki* means 'foot' in Malay). Traditionally, it is used for de-husking padi. It is also used to pound the batter used for making Lem Peng, a near-extinct Chinese New Year speciality.

Here are some tips for pounding *rempah* with a *lesong*:

Do the pounding with the *lesong* placed on the floor.

Place a thick layer of old newspaper or cloth under the mortar to protect the floor and also to minimise the transmission of noise to the floor below if you live in an apartment.

To be seated comfortably when pounding *rempah*, use a *bung ku* or low stool.

As there will be considerable splashing of the *rempah*, line the area surrounding the mortar with old newspapers. I use one hand to cover the mortar to minimise splashing. The Thais have invented an attachment for the pestle to prevent splashing.

Start by pounding the dry spice ingredients individually before the wet spices. This will ensure that each dry spice has been pounded till they are sufficiently fine.

In addition to pounding downwards at the centre of the mortar, pound at an angle away from the centre, going around the mortar to ensure that all the *rempah* is pounded uniformly.

Use a teaspoon to regularly scrape the *rempah* from the top and sides of the mortar and move it to the centre.

My rule of thumb for deciding when to stop pounding is when you cannot see any whole chilli seed in the *rempah*.

I find that using a good food processor for grinding *rempah* saves a lot of the hassle of pounding – but only if the *rempah* is to be fried.

For Nonya Sambal Belacan which is not cooked, there is a distinct difference between that prepared by a food processor and that prepared using the *lesong*. The difference is less discernable if the Sambal Belacan is partially pounded before being ground in a food processor, especially when large quantities are involved.

My cousin Sandy advised me a long time ago to use chillies with wrinkled skin and not chillies with smooth skin for making *rempah*, but I didn't take heed of her advice. After pounding a fair amount of *rempah* over the years, I have realised that the smooth skin of chillies will not break up even after a lot of pounding. I have got the message, but, unfortunately, one does not have much choice in buying smooth or wrinkled chillies these days!

Cheok Bo (Rice Grinder)

Rice, together with coconut, are the two most important ingredients in Nonya cooking. Today's generation is familiar with the white cooked rice but may not know the difference between the uncooked polished and unpolished rice, not to mention padi – the unhusked rice. Hence, it is useful to recall some traditional practices related to rice and to explain its planting, harvesting, and processing.

It wasn't that long ago that padi was grown in Malacca. There were also padi fields on the side of the road from Georgetown to the airport at Bayan Lepas in Penang. Those who have ventured to Kedah will know that it is the rice-bowl of Malaysia.

Rice is a wild grass that was domesticated most probably in the Yangtze river valley in China about 5000 BC. Padi fields have to be flooded for a few weeks before rice seedlings are transplanted in them. After harvesting, the rice is threshed to separate the grains from the stalk. In the old days, the wooden *lesong kaki* was used to pound the padi to separate the husk from the rice grain. A round, bamboo sieve, called a *nyiru*, was used in the winnowing process to separate the brown rice from the chaff or husk. Brown rice

LESONG OF DIFFERENT SIZES SIT ATOP A PULUT TAITAI BOX (SEE PAGE 231).

is milled to obtain the polished rice that we buy from the supermarkets today.

Rice can be classified by grain shape – long, medium, or short. In general, long-grain rice is grown in tropical climates while short- and medium-grain rice are grown in cooler climates, eg in Japan, Korean, Italy, and Spain. Round-grain rice, when cooked, is more sticky than the fluffier, long-grain rice.

In Southeast Asia, rice also comes in different colours: transparent polished rice, glutinous rice which is whiter and less transparent, red rice, black glutinous rice, and brown rice. Brown rice refers to unpolished rice which has not been milled; it is nutritionally healthier and more expensive! Glutinous rice is a cultivar specially bred to be sticky and dense. It is does not contain gluten – the glutinous in its name refers to its stickiness. It is often steamed and used for desserts. Black glutinous rice is neither black (it is more deep purple) nor glutinous. As it is not milled, it has a crunchy texture. It is used for Pulut Hitam, the cooked-rice dessert which is served with coconut milk.

It was a common practice in my younger days to pick out the unhusked padi from the rice before washing and cooking. We called this *pilih beras*, literally, to choose padi. Rice then was threshed and unhusked manually, hence padi could be mixed with the polished rice. Today, it is unusual to find padi in polished rice although one can still find grains of unhusked rice in brown or unpolished rice.

In the past, there was also a significant amount of polished rice mixed with glutinous rice, so one had to pick out the polished rice, especially if the glutinous rice was to be steamed. Glutinous rice cooks faster than polished rice. Thus, if polished rice were not removed, they would be undercooked and spoil the texture of the glutinous rice in savoury dishes such as Bak Chang (rice dumplings), Kee Chang, Nasi Kunyit, and Rempah Udang, and desserts like Pulut Taitai and Pulut Inti.

The sorting of rice was done on a large, brass or enamel tray called *dulang*. For the sake of research, I sorted through 1 kilogram of glutinous rice and found only three grams of non-glutinous rice or 0.3 percent, so the presence of polished rice in glutinous rice is not apparently such a problem today. Still, we have to be vigilant.

Ground glutinous rice is used extensively in Asian, especially Nonya, cooking. A long list of Nonya cakes like Cheak Bee Soh, Kueh Ee, Kueh Kosui, Kow Chan Kuih, Ondeh Ondeh and Kueh Koci use ground glutinous rice. On the other hand, ground polished rice is the main ingredient for Putu Mayam, Apong, Apong Balek and the *bee hoon* (*bor*) that goes with Laksa.

Today, we just go out to the shops to buy the ground rice when we need it. In the old days, the rice had to be ground from scratch, using a *cheok bo*.

The *cheok bo* is made up of two cylindrical blocks of granite. The bottom piece has a moat with a spout, and a square hole in the middle. The top cylinder has, off centre, a round hole going through from top to bottom. A wooden handle is fixed to the side of the top portion to turn it while a wooden or metal peg with a square bottom and a cylindrical top joins the square and round holes in the top and bottom parts of the *cheok bo*. This is to keep the top block in place while it is rotated.

Rice or other grains to be ground, mixed with water, is fed through the hole on top. The grain is ground between the two surfaces as the top piece is rotated. Like the *batu giling*, there are tiny grooves on the surfaces of the granite to facilitate the milling of the rice as it is moved round and round and away from the centre towards the sides. The liquid flows into the moat and is drained through the spout. A cloth bag is attached to the spout to collect the wet, ground rice. The bag is then hung up to drain away the water and obtain a fairly dry paste.

Traditionally, flour sacks were recycled and sewn into smaller bags for this purpose because the weave of the cloth is just right to drain the water and leave the ground rice in the bag. The same cloth was also used to make bags for squeezing *santan* (coconut milk) from grated coconuts. Today, one would use muslin.

Kacip (Areca Nut Cutter)

The *kacip* is a tool for slicing *pinang* (areca nut). Its proper name is *kacip pinang* or *kacip sireh pinang*. *Sireh* is the leaf chewed with the *pinang*. Penang is named after this nut, and the *pinang* tree is part of Penang's state flag.

The *kacip* is used not only in the Malaysian Peninsula but also in India, Sri Lanka, Indonesia, Thailand, and in the islands and the lands surrounding the Indian and Pacific Oceans (excluding the Americas) where the chewing of *pinang* is prevalent.

The *kacip* can be better described as a hand guillotine rather than a pair of scissors. It is made of a sharp blade with a handle moving against a flat surface also with a handle attached, the fulcrum being in front of the blade. The blade, made of forged iron, is extremely sharp. I find it especially useful for removing the husk from the *pinang* and to slice the nut most finely.

Most *kacip* have intricate designs of animals and floral motifs, and some are decorated in gold or silver.

During the Mooncake Festival, you will find *lengkok* (water calthrope) in the markets. *Lengkok* looks like a flying bat or buffalo's head and horns. It must be boiled before it can be eaten. I found it rather difficult to remove the black shell of this nut until I found that the *kacip* is a very convenient tool for slicing off the hard shell.

Chopper and Chopping Board

The chopper or cleaver is one of the most useful and versatile knives in the Nonya kitchen. In the old days, when it was customary to hire a *chong por* (chef) to come to the house to prepare a feast to celebrate a wedding or birthday, he would come with an assistant or two armed with choppers. They used the chopper for virtually everything, from slicing, chopping, and cutting vegetables, meat and seafood. They minced meat with two choppers, and even opened tin cans with just a few strokes of a chopper!

Graters

A brass grater was traditionally used to shred root vegetable like *bangkwang* (jicama) and tapioca. However, the old nonyas would not use this shredder because the results are not uniform compared to their slicing with a knife.

This type of shredder is still being sold in shops today, but there are also mandolines which does a good job of very fine slicing. My mother had a wooden mandoline; I have one made of plastic from the same Japanese manufacturer. It is very sharp and can julienne root vegetables in three sizes faster than slicing with a knife or chopper. It has the seal of approval from my cousin Sandy who uses it regularly to make Poh Piah.

Tools for Grilled Cuttlefish

In the old days, dried *jiu hu* or cuttlefish was eaten after it has been grilled over charcoal then stretched and softened by pounding.

ACCOUTREMENTS AND INGREDIENTS FOR CHEWING BETEL NUT, INCLUDING THE *KAPIT*. THE DAB OF WHITE PASTE IN THE BOWL IS SLAKED LIME.

To toast *jiu hu*, a grill with two metal nets held together by hinges was used. The cuttlefish was kept flat between the nets while it was grilled over a charcoal fire. The hot *jiu hu* was then rolled up tightly and pounded with a hammer on a small metal platform cut off an I-beam used in building construction.

I went looking for the wire mesh grill for toasting the cuttlefish but could not find one. Finally, I decided to make my own from scratch. I used thin stainless steel wire to make chicken mesh for the body and thick wire for the frame, and made a grill like the ones we used years ago.

For the I-beam, I went straight to a metal shop. I asked them to cut a section of about 30 cm and file off the edges. I thought I could tidy it up myself, but after a lot of filling and using a lot of sandpaper, I brought it back to the shop to get the working surface of the I-beam polished. A hammer from a hardware store completed my tools for pounding cuttlefish the way it was done when I was young. You can use a mortar and pestle to pound the cuttlefish, but the result is not quite the same.

Fortunately, *hung lor* or charcoal stoves are still readily available. Of course you can also grill over a barbecue or a Satay grill.

The Jiu Hu Eng Chye stalls were the early adopters of mechanical rollers for stretching cuttlefish. The machine consists of two rollers, with the bottom one connected to a handle to rotate it. A knob at the top controls the space between the rollers and thus the thickness of the rolled *jiu hu*. My sister brought one of these rollers in Thailand.

With these mechanical rollers, *jiu hu* can be stretched more uniformly, thinly and faster than pounding using a hammer or *lesong*. I have not seen an electrically powered cuttlefish roller but I am certain they exist because they are not much different from the larger electric rollers used for extracting sugarcane juice.

Ice Shavers

In my school days, ice was manually shaved using a large blade mounted on a wooden block, very much like a large version of the plane used for shaving wood. For shaving wood, the plane is slid over the wood but, for ice, the shaver is upside-down and a block of ice is slid over the blade and the ice shavings are collected at the bottom of the shaver.

MY HOMEMADE MESH GRILL FOR TOASTING CUTTLEFISH.

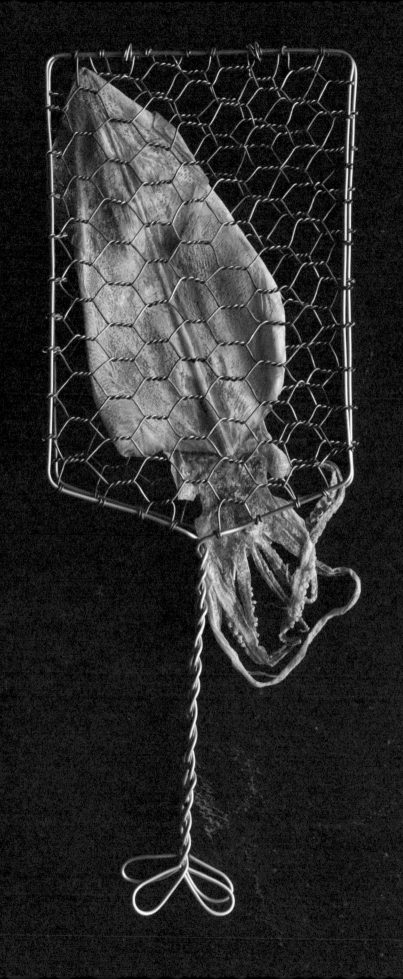

A small, wooden block with nails embedded is used to give a good grip on the ice block and to prevent the hand from freezing. I bought one of these shavers in a market in Phnom Penh.

Over the years, ice shavers have evolved into sophisticated mechanical and electrical machines we have today.

When I searched the Internet for ice shavers, I came across a large number of ice shavers of the same brand – Swan – many from Japan and some from Taiwan which was ruled by the Japanese for nearly thirty years.

Today, we can buy handy manual or electrical ice shavers for use at home. Some shave ice cubes while others use an electric motor to rotate a small cylindrical block of ice over a blade; for this device, you will have to make your own ice block in your home freezer.

Sugarcane Crusher

In Penang, sugarcane juice was originally sold by Sikhs who used a mechanical crusher to squeeze the sugarcane between two rollers. The bottom roller rotated freely. The upper roller was turned by four handles connected to one of its sides. As the upper roller was turned, sugarcane, which had been cut into two, lengthwise, was forced between the rollers and crushed to squeeze out the juice. The sugarcane juice was collected via a sloping metal tray below the rollers.

Why were these sugarcane juicers operated by Sikhs? I initially thought that it was because they have the physical strength to operate these sugarcane crushers. The truth is that sugarcane is native to India. Indeed, when I visited India, I was struck by the number of stalls selling sugarcane juice.

Nowadays, sugarcane stalls have very compact, electrically driven, sugarcane crushers.

AN ICE SHAVER. THE WOODEN BLOCK WITH NAILS EMBEDDED IS USED TO GRIP THE ICE WHILE SHAVING IT.

Steamed Egg and Minced Meat

SERVES 4-6 IF SERVED WITH OTHER DISHES

This is an old family dish that I remember eating from my childhood. Minced pork is mixed with eggs, soya sauce, preserved radish and steamed. It is a simple and fast dish to prepare. As this dish has Chinese origins, pork is traditionally used but other meat like chicken or beef can be used instead. I mince the meat with the traditional chopping block and a Chinese chopper. Old Hainanese chefs (chong por)*, being experts, chopped with two choppers, one in each hand.*

2 eggs
130 g minced pork
1½ tbps soya sauce
½ tsp sugar
½ tsp sesame oil
Ground pepper, to taste
1 tablespoon preserved
   radish (*tong chai*)
8 half eggshells water
1 stalk spring onions,
   finely sliced

Prepare a wok with a steamer. Pour in enough water to bring the water level to just below the steamer. This will ensure that the water does not dry out before the dish is cooked.

Break the eggs; keep one half of an eggshell for measuring water. Beat up the eggs.

Thoroughly mix the minced pork with the eggs, making sure that the mince is not lumpy. Add the soya sauce, the sugar, sesame oil and ground pepper.

Chop up the preserved radish coarsely and mix with the pork and egg.

Add 8 half eggshells of water gradually, ensuring that the water is well mixed in.

Place the dish in the steamer when the water in the wok is boiling vigourously. Cover. After about 5 minutes, stir the mixture, moving the cooked portion from the centre of the dish to the edge. Check that there is enough water in the steamer. Cover and steam for about another 5 minutes. Stick a fork into the centre of the dish. The dish is cooked if the liquid which runs out is clear.

Alternatively, the dish can be cooked in a microwave oven using the above instructions. The timings have to be modified according to the wattage of the microwave oven.

Garnish with the sliced spring onions.

Steamed Egg with Minced Meat is normally served with rice together with other dishes.

Sambal Heh Bee MINCED DRIED PRAWN SAMBAL

What is Sambal Heh Bee? Is it a dish, a snack, a condiment, or what? It is the sort of food the older Babas and Nonyas took with them when they travelled overseas on holiday in case they didn't like the foreign food, just like carrying a small bottle of soya sauce or Sambal Belacan!

Sambal is Malay for a condiment made up of mainly chillies and belacan, *whilst* heh bee *is dried prawns in Hokkien. In Malacca and Singapore, the dish is known as Sambal Udang Kering – all in Malay –* udang *meaning 'prawn' and* kering *meaning 'dry'. Inspite of the name, Sambal Udang Kering is not normally cooked by the Malays.*

Sambal Heh Bee is prepared by pounding dried prawns and frying it with a spice paste till it is dry. It has a slightly sour flavour because of the tamarind used. A versatile dish, it can be taken with rice or used as a condiment to go with ladies fingers or angle beans in place of Sambal Belacan. It is good for making instant Penang Hokkien Mee by adding the sambal in a stock. I found a recipe in my mother's collection for Sambal Udang Sandwich, made up of four alternate layers of brown and white bread with Sambal Heh Bee in between.

This recipe came from my cousin Sandy who often prepares Sambal Heh Bee as gifts to her relatives.

Sambal Heh Bee

350 g dried prawns
150 g tamarind paste,
soaked
    in 300 ml water

Spice Paste
4 stalks lemongrass
4 cloves garlic, skinned and
    minced
30 g dried chillies, soaked in
    water, seeds removed
150 g shallots, skinned and
    minced
16 g turmeric (*kunyit*)
23 g shrimp paste (*belacan*),
    toasted and broken up

8 tbsps oil
2 pandan leaves, each tied
    into a knot
4 tbsps sugar
1½ tsps salt
10 kaffir lime leaves (*daun
    limau purut*), sliced finely

Remove any shells from the dried prawns.

Soak the tamarind in the water, then squeeze between fingers and thumb and sieve to obtain tamarind liquid. Use ²/₃ of the tamarind liquid to soak the dried prawns for 10 minutes; add more water to cover the dried prawns if required. Set aside the other ¹/₃ for the spice paste.

Drain the soaked dried prawns and pound till fine. I find it more convenient to use a food processor as pounding the dried prawns properly is hard work! Set aside the pounded dried prawns.

Wash the stalks of lemongrass and trim off the roots and the leaves, leaving about 5-6 cm of the white root ends. Slice the root ends finely.

Pound the ingredients for the spice paste starting with the lemongrass and the garlic. Then add the chillies, shallots, turmeric, and the *belacan*. Alternativelys use a blender to grind the spice paste.

Heat up a wok, add the oil and, when hot, fry the pandan leaves. Discard the leaves when they become crispy. Saute the spice paste for at least 10 minutes till fragrant. Then add the reserved tamarind liquid, the sugar, salt, and pounded dried prawns

Fry the Sambal Heh Bee, turning the mixture continuously till it is damp but not dry. This will take about 30 minutes. The lumps in the mixture will become smaller and the colour darken from pale gold to brown. Add the finely sliced kaffir lime leaves at the final minute of frying.

Some people prefer their Sambal Heh Bee damp, others prefer theirs dry. If the dry version is preferred, continue frying till it is dry and crispy. Dry Sambal Heh Bee can keep longer than the damp version.

Acar Awak NONYA PICKLES

Acar *is a Southeast Asian variation of the East Indian pickle. It is pronounced 'archat' by the Penang Nonyas. Acar Awak is one of the more elaborate Penang Nonya acars, more so than the Malay version. It is made with* rempah *(spice paste) together with a large variety of vegetables and fruits, as well as coarsely ground peanuts and toasted sesame seeds. The ingredients are blanched in a vinegar solution, giving them a sourish tang and a crunchy texture in addition to the spiciness from the spice paste.*

Awak *is most probably from a Malay word mispronounced by the Penang Nonyas. Friends from my Penang Heritage Food Facebook group identified* rawak *and* rawet *as two possible Malay words from which* awak *is derived. Rawak means 'random', possibly referring to the random types of vegetable used. I tend to favour* rawet *which means 'lasting or durable', referring to the long shelf life of Acar Awak;* awetan *means 'preserves'.*

According to jee chim, *my wife's aunt, Acar Awak featured prominently in the list of festive dishes served in the* tng tok *or* tok panjang *(long table) of Nonya weddings. It can also be taken as an appetiser.*

There are other Nonya acars made of vegetables like cucumber, or fruits like kalamansi lime and belimbing (Averrhoa bilimbi, a sour fruit related to starfruit) and also green chillies filled with grated young papaya. There are also fish acars using salted fish (tanau hu), *firm-flesh fish clutlets of ikan kurau, and whole small fishes like mullet* (chee yah hu, ikan belanak). *The Penang Nonyas have more varieties of* acar *than Singapore and Malacca.*

The general principle of food preservation in making acar *is to use salt and vinegar to pickle, and to reduce the moisture in the ingredients by sun drying and/or squeezing. Soaking the* acar *ingredients in yellow tumeric oil in some cases also helps in the preservation.*

Traditionally, the ingredients were cut into pieces about 2 cm long and the root vegetables are cut to a thickness of just less than 1 cm. They are then mixed with salt and spread on a dulang and dried in the sun. After being sun dried, each type of ingredient was separately blanched and mixed with the fried rempah.

In this recipe, the ingredients are not sun dried but they are squeezed after blanching to remove as much water as possible. You could use two colanders to squeeze out the water from the blanched vegetables but it is more effective to use a strong piece of cloth to wrap the blanched vegetable and squeeze to remove as much water as possible.

Traditionally, the rempah *is ground into a fine paste using the* batu giling *(see page 27). A* lesong *(page 29) can also be used but the* rempah *will not be as fine. Some brands of food processors can also do a good job of grinding the* rempah.

Acar Awak

500 g cucumbers
200 g cauliflower
200 g white cabbage,
    preferred for their thickness
200 g long beans or French
    beans
250 g carrots
150 g brinjals
20 small shallots
8 red chillies

Pickling Solution
600 ml water
400 ml vinegar
2 tbsps salt
2 tbsps sugar

Spice Paste
2 tbsps tamarind soaked in
    4 tbsps water
30 g dried chilli, soaked in
    water, stalks removed
120 g shallots, peeled and
    cut into pieces
40 g turmeric, skinned and
    coarsely chopped
2 stalks lemongrass, use only
    5 cm (2 in) of the root-
    end, coarsely chopped
4 candlenuts, crushed
4 cloves garlic, skinned and
    coarsely chopped
20 g shrimp paste (*belacan*),
    toasted

150 g peanuts, skinned
150 ml oil (traditionally,
    coconut oil)
3 tbsps salt
9 tbsps sugar
50 g sesame seeds, fried
    without oil till golden

Cutting Vegetables
Cut the cucumber, with skin on, into 4 lengthwise
and remove the soft core. If the cucumber is big, cut
each length into two lengthwise so that the width is
about 1 cm. Then cut the cucumber into lengths of
about 2 cm.

Separate each branch of the cauliflower then cut
them into florets of about 2 cm.

Separate the cabbage leaves. Cut off the leaves on
either side of the stalk, leaving a stalk about 1 cm
wide. Cut the stalks into 2-cm lengths and the leaves
into 2-cm squares.

Top and tail the long beans and break or cut into 2-
cm lengths.

Top and tail the carrots and cut each carrot into
two, lengthwise. Cut each half, lengthwise again into
two, three or four depending on the size, to obtain
a consistent thickness of about 1 cm. Then cut into
lengths of about 2 cm.

Remove the stalk of the brinjal and cut the brinjal
into two, lengthwise. Cut each half, lengthwise, into
two or three to obtain a consistent thickness of about
1 cm. Then cut into lengths of about 2 cm.

Peel the shallots, removing the root portions.

Remove the stalks of the chillies and cut off 2 cm of
the tips. Slice the chillies into two and remove the
seeds. Cut into lengths of about 2 cm. Alternatively,
you could do it the traditional way and slit the
chillies into four from just below the caps.

Pickling Vegetables
Heat the water in a pan and add the vinegar, salt and
sugar when it has boiled.

Add the cucumber to the boiling pickling solution
to blanch for about a minute. Pour the cucumber

into a colander with another pan underneath to collect the pickling solution for reuse. Wrap the cucumber in a muslin cloth and squeeze out as much of the liquid as possible. Unwrap the cloth and spread out the cucumbers on a tray.

Repeat the blanching process for the cauliflower, cabbage, long beans, carrots, brinjals and the shallots. Each vegetable must be blanched separately. The carrots will need a bit more time to blanch.

Assembly
Squeeze the soaked tamarind between your finger and thumb. Use a spoon to pass the tamarind and liquid through a sieve to separate the pulp from the fibre and seeds. Set aside the tamarind liquid.

Pound or grind finely the ingredients for the spice paste. If using a food processor, you may need to add a few tablespoons of water to facilitate the grinding.

Roast the peanuts or fry in a wok till golden brown. Cool and crush or pound the nuts. If a food processor is used, it is better to divide the nuts into two batches, grinding one batch coarser than the other.

Heat up the wok till it is hot. Add the oil and, when it is hot, add the spice paste and fry over a low to medium fire. Stir continuously to ensure that the paste does not stick to the wok. Fry till it is fragrant and the oil separates. This will take at least 15 minutes. Add 2 tablespoons of water if the paste becomes too dry and sticks to the wok.

Mix the tamarind liquid, salt and sugar into the spice paste. Stir in the blanched vegetables and cook for about 2 minutes. Then add in the pounded groundnuts and half of the sesame seeds. Keep the remaining sesame seeds in an airtight bottle and sprinkle on the *acar* when serving.

Let the Acar Awak sit overnight before serving. If the *acar* is to be kept longer, store in clean, dry bottles.

Jiu Hu GRILLED CUTTLEFISH

When I was a child in the days before potato crisps, we had jiu hu which was pounded into long, thin strips and toasted. We called it Sotong Ketok (the Malay word for 'pound' being ketok). The aroma from the toasting attracted customers to the jiu hu stall like no other advertisement could. A small piece of the crispy jiu hu was dipped in a sweet and sour chilli sauce and enjoyed! This was the Malay version that we grew up with at the Chinese Swimming Club at Tanjong Tokong. It was made by a Malay man who also sold Kedah Laksa.

A Facebook friend mentioned, "This Sotong Ketok was only sold when there was any temple celebration and they had the Chinese opera when I was little...." There were certainly many hawker stalls that accompanied the Chinese opera that moved from one temple to another to give performances.

Like so many dried seafood products, dried squid or sotong in Malay was once very cheap compared to today's prices. A small piece of jiu hu cost 5 cents in the old club and probably 10 cents in the new one. Now, 100 g of rolled jiu hu costs nearly RM$10!

In the past, the jiu hu was made by first toasting the dried squid in a wire-mesh grill over a charcoal fire. The hot jiu hu was then rolled up tightly and pounded with a hammer on a section of the I-beam used in building construction. Some families used a lesong (mortar and pestle) but it is not so effective.

The pounded dried squid is unrolled, carefully stretched out, then roasted, rolled up and pounded again. This process is repeated till the sotong gets thinner and longer. If carefully done, the jiu hu can be stretched to about three or four times its original length. The tentacles of the squid are also pounded but they don't expand as much as the body of the squid, and they have a slightly different texture.

The Jiu Hu Eng Chai stalls were the early adopters of mechanical rollers for stretching the dried squid. The bottom roller is connected to a handle to rotate it while the top roller can be adjusted to control the thickness of the jiu hu being rolled. With these mechanical rollers, jiu hu can be stretched more uniformly, thinly and faster than pounding.

My sister brought a roller from Thailand when we were trying to squeeze our own sugarcane juice. It only dawned on me that the roller was meant for jiu hu when I started writing about jiu hu. I have not seen electrically powered rollers, but I am certain they exist because they are not much different from the larger rollers used for squeezing sugarcane for its juice.

Once the jiu hu has been sufficiently stretched, it is cut into smaller pieces and finally grilled. The crispy jiu hu is now ready to be savoured with the chilli sauce.

Nowadays, we can buy rolled jiu hu in different forms. The crispy ones with chilli sauce flavour are made in Penang or Southern Thailand. Other jiu hu tit-bits are moist and untoasted; they could be spiced or plain and are mostly imported from Taiwan.

Jiu Hu

5 dried squids

Sweet & Sour Chilli Sauce
4 tbsps bottled sweet chilli
  sauce
2 tsps light soya sauce
2 tsps lime juice or vinegar
1 tsp sugar
1 tbsp hot water
1 tbsp peanuts, toasted and
  finely pounded

Pounding the Squid
You will need a wire-mesh grill for toasting the dried squid, and a hammer and a thick metal plate for pounding the squid. Alternatively, use a mortar and pestle.

Separate the tentacles from the body of each squid. Place the body of the dried squid in the wire-mesh grill and toast over a charcoal or gas fire till it is supple enough to be rolled up.

Roll it up tightly by the width along the length of the squid. Hammer it hard from end to end. Twist the roll and continue hammering. The squid will begin to become fiberous.

Carefully unroll the squid and stretch it out without breaking it into pieces. Place the stretched squid back in the wire-mesh grill and toast the squid to heat it up without burning it. Tightly roll up the squid again and repeat the hammering process.

Repeat until there are gaps all along the length of the stretched squid. Toast the pounded squid, Similarly, toast each set of the tentacles and hammer them. Toast again and repeat the hammering. Keep the pounded tentacles aside.

Repeat for the other squids.

Cut the stretched squids into smaller pieces to fit the wire-mesh grill. Now toast the cut pieces and the tentacles till crisp. The crispy squid is now ready to be savoured with the sweet and sour chilli sauce.

Store the toasted squid in an air-tight container to keep it crispy, especially in humid climates.

Sauce
Mix together the sweet chilli sauce, light soya sauce, lime juice, sugar, and hot water. Then add the pounded peanuts. Serve with the toasted squid.

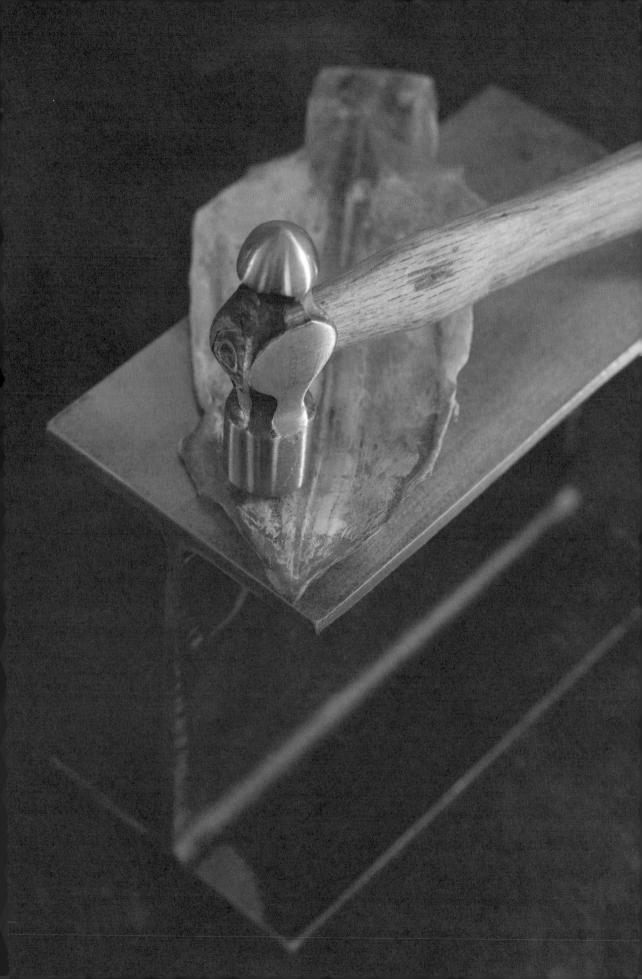

Keropok PRAWN CRACKERS

Keropok is native to the Malay Peninsula. It is made from prawns or fish. My mother used a lesong (mortar and pestle) to pound the prawns and whole peppercorns. Tapioca flour is added and the mixture is kneaded into a dough. It is easier to use a food processor and even easier if the processor can do the kneading. The colour of the keropok depends on the prawns used. The darker-shelled prawns will give an orangy colour. Fish keropok is dark grey before frying but, after deep-frying, there isn't much difference between the colours of the prawn and fish keropok. Keropok is commonly sold and served as a snack. More recently, it has been used to garnish roasted chicken and Inche Kabin.

600 g prawns, shelled and deveined
4 tsps salt
1 tbsp ground pepper
450 g tapioca flour
1 tbsp baking powder
Water

Pound the prawns and mix with the salt and pepper to form a paste.

Sieve the flour and baking powder and mix it with the prawn paste. Knead to form a dough. Add more tapioca flour if too wet or more water if too dry. The dough should not stick to your hands. Form into rolls about 3 cm in diameter.

Steam for at least 30 minutes till the rolls have bloated. That's why it is important that there should be sufficient space between the rolls of *keropok* in the steamer tray. When the *keropok* rolls have cooled down, keep them in the refrigerator over-night.

Cut the rolls of *keropok* into round slices of about 2 mm thick. If you prefer large pieces of *keropok*, slice at a slant for an elliptical shape.

Spread the sliced *keropok* on a tray and dry them in the sun for at least two days. Turn the *keropok* over regularly when you move the tray about to catch the sun. The *keropok* will shrink and become quite hard when they are dried. Keep in a sealed plastic bag.

To deep fry the *keropok*, heat oil in a wok. When the oil is smoking hot, put in a few *keropok*s at a time. Remove with a seive when they have fully expanded but before they turn golden brown.

The fried *keropok* should be stored in an air-tight container if there is any left-over to keep!

Kuih Ee GLUTINOUS RICE BALLS

Kuih Ee is a Chinese festive dish prepared to mark the Winter Solstice or Dong Zhi Festival in the northern hemisphere when the night is longest and the day is shortest. Falling on 21 or 22 December each year, it marks the turning point between winter and spring; a crucial date for farmers, afterwhich they have to prepare for planting. When we were young, we were told that we shall be one year older after eating Kuih Ee.

Kuih Ee is made from a dough of ground glutinous rice. Small portions of the dough are rolled into balls which are boiled in water and then served in a ginger-flavoured syrup. The bigger Kuih Ee, sometimes referred to as ibu *or mother, are white while the smaller ones are red. The Kuih Ee of the Hokkiens do not have any filling. However, other Chinese dialect groups include sweet fillings like ground peanuts, red beans and black sesame. These can be found in frozen form in supermarkets today. There is also a savoury version of Kuih Ee. Onde Ondeh (page 90) is a related snack.*

In the past, the process of grinding rice was labourious and time-consuming, taking several days. After normal rice was sorted out from glutinous rice, the latter had to be soaked in water before being ground in a stone grinder known as cheok bo *in Hokkien (see page 31). The liquid ground rice was then channelled into* mee hoon tay *(literally translated: wheat flour bag), the cloth bags used to import flour from mainly Australia. The bag of ground glutinous rice had to be hung up overnight to drain off the excess water.*

The preparation of Kuih Ee today is quite straight-forward since the main ingredient, ground glutinous rice flour, is so readily available. Making dough from this is a quick process. However, it is better to leave the dough aside to properly absorb the water for at least 30 minutes. Jee chim, my wife's aunt, gave us her tip: a bit of sugar should be added to make the Kuih Ee softer.

In Malaysia and Singapore, you can buy Kuih Ee dough in the market a day before the Winter Solstice. In the Pulau Tikus Market in Penang, stalls were selling glutinous rice dough of various colours: White, red, yellow, green, and even brown! I don't remember so many colours of Kuih Ee in my young days; I remember only white and red. A packet of the dough cost just over RM$5. One stall holder claimed that her dough had no normal rice although I am not sure how the presence of normal rice will affect the texture of Kuih Ee.

The rolling of Kuih Ee is a fun activity for the family, especially younger children. The Hokkien term is soh Kuih Ee *or to roll the dumpling.*

I recently came across the Teochew Kuih Ee called Hooi Lye Nyee. The ee is fashioned into a cube instead of a ball, otherwise the preparation is the same. This style of ee symbolises the fullfuillment of all ambitions based on the proverb zhi zai si fang [志在四方] *which translates as to 'travel to all corners of the world to make one's mark'. The connection is the pun on the character* fang [方], *which means both 'directions' and 'square', the latter referring to the cube.*

Kuih Ee

Dough
½ tsp sugar
190 ml water
200 g glutinous rice flour
20 drops red colouring or
    to your preference

Syrup
1 litre water
150 g sugar
30 g ginger, skinned and
    sliced coarsely (optional)
4 pandan leaves, knotted

Dough
Dissolve the sugar in the water. Sieve the glutinous rice flour into a mixing bowl and gradually add the sugared water, stirring continuously. The dough is ready when it comes off the sides of the bowl. You may not need all the water specified in the recipe, so do not use up all the water if the dough is too wet. The dough has a shiny, wet look if there is too much water, in which case you need to add more glutinous rice flour.

Divide the dough into two equal portions. Add the red colouring to one portion and knead thoroughly so that the colour is uniform. Keep the dough covered or transfer into a plastic bag. Set aside to allow the flour to absorb the water. The dough can be prepared earlier and stored in the refrigerator.

Syrup
Boil the water, add the sugar and the ginger and the pandan leaves. Simmer for about 5 minutes to allow the flavour of the ginger to seep into the syrup.

Rolling the Kuih Ee
The dough should be brought back to room temperature if it has been kept in the refrigerator.

Knead both portions of the dough. Roll each portion of dough into a cylinder and cut off small portions. For the white dough, the size of the Kuih Ee is bigger – about 2 cm and the red ones should be smaller – just over 1 cm. Roll each small piece of dough between the palms of your hands to form a round ball. Repeat for all the dough. Place the balls on a tray and cover with a cloth.

Boil a generous amount of water in a pot. Transfer the white Kuih Ee into the boiling water. Fish out the balls with a seive when they float, and drop them in a prepared bowl of cold water. When the white Kuih Ees have been done, do the same for the red Kuih Ee.

Serve, either hot or cold, a mixture of white Kuih Ees and red ones with the syrup in individual bowls.

Ice Kacang FILLED SHAVED ICE CONES

Ice Kacang is a refreshing cold dessert partaken between and after meals especially in the hot, tropical climate.

Shaved ice, as a dessert, is likely to have originated from a region or civilisation where there was snow and ice close by. It has a long history in Japan and has been recorded since Roman times. So, it is surprising that when we served Ice Kacang to our English friends in London, it wasn't well received!

For countries nearer the equator, consignments of ice were brought by ships to busy ports like Singapore, Penang and Malacca, before ice was made locally. Hoo Ah Kay, or popularly known as Whampoa, was a Singapore merchant who operated an ice house in Clark Quay by the Singapore River. He started shipping ice in 1854 from the New England states of America. In fact, Henry Thoreau, in Walden, *his famous meditation on simple living, wrote about ice from Walden Pond being exported to the East. Surprisingly, Whampoa left the ice business two years later because of a lack of demand.*

Ang Tow Sng is Hokkien for Ice Kacang. From the name, you can tell that the main ingredients are ang tow *(red beans) and* sng *(ice, or shaved ice, to be precise). More recently, it has acquired a more exotic Malay name – ABC or Air Batu Campur –* air batu *is literally 'water stone', and* campur *means 'mix'. Ice is also known as* ais *in Malay.*

The basic Ice Kacang would have a few teaspoons of ang tow *in a bowl topped with ice shavings. The red beans are boiled with sugar till they are soft. Later versions of Ice Kacang have other ingredients which are now considered traditional:* attap chee *(seeds of the attap palm in syrup),* jagong *(tinned creamed sweet corn),* leong fun *or* cin chau *(grass jelly),* cendol *jelly, raisins, and agar agar. In Penang, shredded sweetened nutmeg is also added.*

Syrups of different flavours and colours are drizzled over the compacted ice shavings followed by evaporated milk. The red one was rose flavoured while the brown one was sarsi (sarsaparilla) flavoured. There were also syrups coloured green and yellow. In the past, we could choose the flavour of the syrup we liked on our Ice Kacang.

Today, all sorts of other ingredients like ice cream, pounded peanuts and tinned mix fruits are added to Ice Kacang, partly to inflate the price and for novelty. Gula Melaka syrup is also popular. Unfortunately, the large red kidney beans are now often used instead of the traditional small red beans.

Ice Kacang is served at road-side hawker stalls and kopitiam *(coffeeshops). There was a stall parked just outside my grandmother's house in Macalister Road; pity I was too young then to have tried the Ice Kacang there. An up-market and expensive Ice Kacang is still served at Kek Seng Kopitiam in Penang Road. In the days when a bowl of Ice Kacang costs 20 cents, those served at Kek Seng cost over two dollars each. You could order the dessert with* ang tow *or* jagong *and two scoops of ice cream of your choice. The popular ice cream flavours were durian*

and jagong. *My mother usually ordered* angelok – *a jelly made from ground almond. In Singapore, there was a famous stall in the now demolished Koek Lane that drizzled only red syrup and evaporated milk over their Ice Kacang.*

Before the advent of machines, ice was manually shaved using a large blade mounted on a wooden block, very much like a large version of the plane used for shaving wood. A small block of wood with multiple nails was employed to obtain a better grip on the ice as it is slid over the blade. The ice shavings were collected at the bottom of the shaver. I have seen such ice shavers still on sale in Cambodia.

We can now buy ice shavers for use at home. There is a handy and easy-to-use one which shaves ice cubes. Another has an electric motor which rotates a small cylindrical block of rice over a blade; for this device you will have to make your own ice block in your freezer.

In the days before refrigerators were common at home, ice in Malaya and Singapore were made in ice factories and delivered by lorry to distributors in towns. There was an ice distributor's store at the junction of Bangkok Lane and Burmah Road in Pulau Tikus, Penang. The Singapore Ice Works was established along Sungei Road in the late 1950s. I remember blocks of ice about 1 x 2 x 3 feet (30 x 60 x 90 cm) being delivered. Sharp metal hooks and pincers were used to manoeuvre the heavy blocks from the lorry down a wooden plank onto the road. A long saw was used to score the ice and then a small block of wood was used to hit the saw much like how a mason would cut up bricks. In this way, the ice was quickly chopped into smaller blocks. The ice was then stored in large boxes filled with sawdust for insulation. I have seen blocks of ice being off-loaded from a lorry in a market in Phom Penh. Instead of a wooden plank, a mechanical chute guided the ice blocks down onto the road.

Sawdust and gunnysacks were very effective in keeping ice from melting even in tropical temperatures. Sawdust was phased out when people were concerned about it being a health hazard as sawdust was re-cycled by drying it out on the road. But then, so were other dry products like ikan bilis and salted fish!

A block of ice about 6 x 6 x 8 inches (15 x 15 x 20 cm) cost about 20 cents in the 1950s. The ice block would be covered in sawdust, wrapped in old newspaper and tied up with a piece of kiam chow *(marsh reed) commonly used then for tying virtually everything in days before rafia strings.*

Desserts similar to Ice Kacang can be found in many countries in East Asia. Sweetened red beans, syrups and evaporated or condensed milk are used in the local versions in Japan (Kakigõri), Korea (Patbingsu), Taiwan (Bàobìng), and Phillipines (Halo-halo). This strongly suggests that Ice Kacang originated in East Asia, probably in Japan.

Ice Kacang

Red Beans
50 g red beans, soaked in
   water for about 4 hours
200 ml water
50 g sugar

Agar Agar
200 ml water
8 g agar agar
50 g sugar
½ tsp rose essence

Syrups
400 ml water
400 g sugar
½ tsp red food colouring
1 tsp rose essence
1 tsp sarsaparilla essence

Small tin of evaporated milk
Ice cream (optional)

150 g grass jelly, cut into
   thin strips
150 g *cendol* jelly (see page 101)
50 g raisins
50 g shredded sweetned
   nutmeg
100 g attap seeds in syrup
200 g creamed sweet corn

Red Beans
Rinse the pre-soaked red beans. Put them in 200 ml of water and bring to a boil. Then simmer for at least 30 minutes till the beans are soft. Add the sugar and more water if it is too dry. Bring to a boil again and simmer for about 5 minutes. The beans should be easily mashed but still whole.

Agar Agar
Heat up the water and dissolve the agar agar and sugar. Bring to a boil. When the jelly is cool but not even partially set, stir in the rose essence and pour the jelly into a tray. Place in the refrigerator to harden. Cut up the agar-agar into thin strips similar to the grass jelly.

Syrups
Boil the water and dissolve the sugar in it. When the syrup has cooled down, divide the syrup into two portions.

Add the red food colouring and the rose essence to one portion of the syrup and mix in the sarsaparilla essence to the other portion. It is best to keep these syrups in air-tight bottles.

Evaporated Milk
Punch two small holes opposite one another on the edge of the evaporated milk tin to drizzle the milk.

Assembly
Scoop one or two teaspoonful of each of the following ingredients into a bowl: the red beans, agar agar, grass jelly, *cendol* jelly, raisins, shredded sweetened nutmeg, and about 3 attap seeds.

Add a generous amount of shaved ice over these ingredients. You need to compact the shaved ice otherwise the ice will melt too quickly.

Pour the syrup uniformly over the ice using your preferred colours and flavours. Drizzle the evaporated milk over the Ice Kacang and finish by adding a teaspoonful or two of the creamed sweet corn, and ice cream if you wish.

Ice Balls

Most Ice Kacang stalls in my youth also sold Ice Balls or Ais Kepal in Malay. A basic Ice Ball is made by compacting shaved ice into a ball and drizzling on the same syrups used for Ice Kacang. You can ask for a filling of red beans, the syrup of your choice, or even two syrups – one on each half of the Ice Ball.

In those days, an Ice Ball costs only about 5 to 10 cents. In the early noughties, the Ice Kacang stall at Swatow Lane made an Ice Ball for me and charged me one dollar even though it did not have red beans inside. It melted very quickly in my hands; I don't remember having such a problem in my young days. I am sure that it was because the ice was not compacted enough. Now, there is a stall in Armenian street selling Ice Balls to tourists for several dollars!

I have many memories of Ice Balls. When I was small, it was not uncommon for children to suck the Ice Balls till they were white and then persuaded the Ice Ball seller to pour on more syrup. Then there was the one who ate Ice Balls against her mother's advice but was found out because of the coloured syrup stains left on her hands. I do remember Ice Balls made with a loop of kiam chow incorporated in each so that they could be held by the string without having to touch the Ice Ball!

Making Ice Balls

I find the best way of making an Ice Ball is to over-fill a small bowl with shaved ice and to compress the ice tightly, then adding more ice and compacting it till a nice sphere is formed.

To make Ice Balls with filling, fill a bowl with ice and compress it. Then make a hole in the centre and put in the sweetened red beans or any of the Ice Kacang ingredients. Add more shaved ice and compress, repeating till you have formed a ball.

Remove the Ice Ball from the bowl and drizzle syrup and some evaporated milk over it.

Place on an empty glass for serving.

Sugarcane Juice

The juice squeezed out of sugarcane is a thirst quencher in the hot, equatorial climate of Malaysia and Singapore. The juice ranges from yellow to brownish green depending on the type of sugarcane used. In the old days, it was more common to dilute sugarcane juice with water and ice. In more recent times, it is served with a generous amount of ice. As an option, lime can be added to your sugarcane juice.

In the past, the sugarcane was crushed using two mechanical rollers operated manually. In more recent times more compact electically driven crushers can squeeze the last drop of juice out of the sugarcane.

You can make sugarcane juice at home!

Remove the skin of the sugarcane and chop the sugarcane into 5 cm lengths. Cut each section into quarters, lengthwise.

Half fill a blender with the prepared sugarcane and ½ cup of water. Do not use a juicer because the sugarcane is very fiberous. Strain the juice from the sugarcane pulp through a muslin cloth and also squeeze it to extract more juice. Add a little more water and blend, strain and squeeze again. Repeat for the remaining sugarcane.

Serve the sugarcane juice with ice or chilled in the fridge. You may wish to squeeze in some lime juice to taste.

Preparing, Grating & Scraping Coconuts

Nonya and Malay food would be vastly different if there were no coconut trees in Southeast Asia. Virtually all parts of the coconut tree can be used for food, as utensils or as accessories for preparing food.

Depending on the species, a coconut ranges from about 12 cm to 25 cm wide with a height of about 15 cm to 30 cm. They grow in bunches of about ten in the crown of a palm tree.

What is normally sold in the shops or supermarket shows the endocarp which is the hard shell of the coconut; most of the husk or the mesocarp had already been removed. The size and shape of a coconut depends on where it originates from. In Southeast Asia, most of the husked coconuts are nearly round. The round ones available in UK supermarkets are from Sri Lanka or India while the elliptical ones are from Africa.

The endocarp encloses the coconut flesh or the endosperm. There is a dark, thin layer surrounding the flesh. This layer is normally removed if the grated coconut is to be served fresh with Nonya or Malay *kuih*s. In the markets of Southeast Asia, this is described as white grated coconut. The dark layer can be left intact if the grated coconut is to be used for squeezing *santan*, the coconut milk used for cooking.

The volume within the flesh or kernel contains coconut water. It is completely full for a young coconut which has soft, jelly-like flesh. The amount of coconut water decreases as the coconut matures and the flesh hardens. So, it is advisable to shake the coconut to check that it has water in it before buying it. Be warned: coconuts without water are rotten. Coconut water should not be confused with coconut milk, which is the white liquid squeezed from grated coconut flesh.

GRATING A COCONUT USING A *KUKUR KELAPA*, THE MALAY NAME FOR A GRATER ATTACHED TO A SADDLE.

71

Coconut Flesh

Fresh, grated, hard coconut flesh is an indispensable ingredient for *kuih*s such as Kuih Kosui, Uwa Kuih, Ondeh Ondeh, Putu Piring, Putu Mayam, and Abok Abok. When slowly fried, we have *kerisik* and Sesargon. *Inti* is what we get when grated coconut is cooked with *gula Melaka. Inti* is the filling for Pulut Inti, Kuih Koci and Kuih Koci Santan, the last of which is similar to Kuih Bongkong.

When grated coconut is squeezed, we get coconut milk. It is an important ingredient for *kuih*s like Pulut Taitai, Pulut Inti, Kuih Bengka, and Kuih Lapis, and Kaya (egg and coconut custard), as well as desserts like Sago Pudding, Cendol and Pulut Hitam.

Coconut milk is also used in cooking rice to give the characteristic *lemak* (creamy) texture of Nasi Lemak and Nasi Kunyit. Similarly, coconut milk is added to curries like Curry Kapitan, and Indian fish curry. *Santan* is an indispensable ingredient in the Nonya Laksa Lemak from Singapore and the similar Curry Laksa from Malaysia.

Coconut Oil

Coconut oil is used in cooking curries by the Nonyas and Malays. My mother used to make her own coconut oil from *santan* squeezed from older coconuts. This coconut milk is heated in a wok over a low fire until a clear, yellow and fragrant virgin coconut oil is left. I should emphasise the low heat used to ensure that the fatty acids in the coconut oil are not destroyed.

I have seen recipes for Mee Siam which include instructions for making the coconut oil from scratch so that the residue from making coconut oil can be used as a condiment for the dish.

Homemade coconut oil is very different from the commercially produced ones which were sold, in the old days, at the *chai tiama* to fuel lamps. Like the many oils we can buy today, coconut oil, made from copra, is industrially processed.

Coconut oil that has not been industrially processed is good for us. Recent studies suggest that the high lauric acid content of virgin coconut oil builds up the body's immunity much like mother's milk. Similarly, non-processed, fresh coconut milk, and grated coconut have positive effects on our health. The saturated fat in coconut is 64 percent of medium-chain fatty acids. These acids are broken down and used mainly to provide energy for the body, and are seldom deposited as fat in the body unlike the long-chain fatty acids.

Besides its many uses as food products such as cooking oil, condiments, pastries, and margarine, extract from copra is used in the manufacture of personal grooming products and a large variety of industrial applications. The residue, which is rich in protein, is used in animal feed.

Coconut Water

Coconut water from a young coconut makes a refreshing drink. Water from mature coconuts are traditionally used for the preparation of various *kuih*s like Coconut Candy, Apong, and Apong Bekuah.

Tapping Coconut Inflorescents

The sap collected from incising the flower clusters of the coconut tree can be made into several edible products like palm sugar (*gula Melaka*), toddy, arrack, vinegar, and yeast.

To make palm sugar, the fresh sap is boiled to obtain a syrup, or boiled further and traditionally poured into bamboo sections to solidify into cylindrical blocks. This dark brown *gula Melaka* is much healthier than processed sugar. Similar products can be obtained from the palmyra palm which is common in Indo-China and India, and the nipah palm.

Gula Melaka is used as a syrup in Cendol, Ice Kacang, and Sago Pudding. In crystaline form, it is used in the filling of Ondeh Ondeh, Abok Abok, and Putu Piring. It also goes well with Putu Mayam.

If left to ferment, the sap would become toddy, used in many old recipes in place of yeast as a rising agent. Further fermentation of toddy gives rise to vinegar while distillation of toddy produces the alcoholic spirit, arrack.

Toddy is a sour brew with not a very pleasant smell – a poor man's alcoholic drink. It used to be sold at government-controlled establishments all over Malaya and Singapore. I recall buying toddy for my mother at the toddy store at Pulau Tikus. In the process, I had to steer clear of the customers who had too much toddy to drink. Interestingly, my cousin had the same experience in Singapore. Some of these shops in Malaysia are still selling toddy today.

Husking Coconuts

As we had coconut trees in our garden in Penang, we had regular visits from two Indians who came to harvest the coconuts for us. They were each equipped with a ring made from coir. To climb the tree, they wrapped the ring round the trunk and used it to support their ankles as they hoisted themselves up the tree.

They carried up a sickle with a long handle, which they used to trim the coconut leaves and to slice off the whole bunch of coconut.

Once the coconuts have been harvested, the task of husking began. The coconut husker is like a fat spear – the blunt, wooden base planted in the ground with the blade pointing up. The coconut is speared on the blade and the husk is removed by leverage. Not much force is needed.

The dried coconut husks have all sorts of uses. I have heard that they were burnt on the covers of Kuih Bahulu moulds to heat them up. It is good for growing orchids and for marcotting plants.

Cracking Coconuts

I have seen so many amusing TV programmes showing how to break open a coconut. To do it the right way, all you need is a heavy chopper.

A husked coconut has what looks like two eyes and a mouth; it looks like a monkey's head! Hold the coconut with the 'face' facing sideways. Use the blunt side of a chopper to hit the coconut hard along the diameter. You may need a second or third blow to fully crack the coconut into two halves. That is how I was taught to crack a coconut.

The 'mouth' of the coconut is the weakest part of the coconut; the shoot of the coconut plant grows through this point. Its condition gives a good indication of the freshness of the coconut. It should be clean and dry. If this area is damp or wet you might as well throw the coconut away.

We can buy young coconuts imported from Thailand these days. Young coconuts have softer shells, but for export they most probably picked a coconut species with harder shells. Hence, even though the coconuts are young they have hard shells.

Grating Coconuts

The flesh of a mature coconut is traditionally grated using what is known in Malay as *kukur kelapa*. It is shaped like a small wooden horse with a serrated metal grater attached to its neck. One sits astride the saddle with the grater in front. Holding half a coconut in one's palms, one scrapes the flesh against the grater. Graters of this type were originally carved out of a block of wood. Today, there is a version designed to fold up and packed away flat.

Most market stalls today use an electric rotating grater. The coconut is broken into

VARIOUS SCRAPERS, NEW AND VINTAGE, FOR SCRAPING THE FLESH FROM COCONUTS.

halves. The storekeeper holds the half coconut and grates it by pressing the flesh against the grater. He has to stop grating before the grater touches the coconut shell because, for grated coconuts which are to be eaten raw with *kuih*, we do not want the black bits from the shell. Younger mature coconuts are preferred for *kuih*s because the shell is yellow – producing, at worst, yellow flecks – and the flesh is less oily.

There is another electrical machine used for grating coconut. It consists of two rotating graters. To use it, the flesh of the coconut must be removed from the shell so that pieces of flesh can be dropped into the grater.

Gratings from the *kikur* is considered too coarse for desserts by the elder Nonyas. Instead, they use a *parut,* a wooden block with short, thin brass wires implanted in it. Another version, which can still be bought today, is a galvanized steel board with barbs cut from the metal. My cousin gave me the one used by my aunt. The one I bought a few years ago is virtually the same, except for the size.

The flesh of the coconut is first removed from the shell by using a curved, rounded blade. The flesh is then grated using the *parut*. Great care should be taken to ensure that your fingers do not get grated too!

I came across a simple and useful grater during a trip to Cambodia. The lady who was using it in the market allowed us to try it out when we asked her about it. I made one for myself by screwing a beer bottle cap onto a wooden handle.

Scrapping Young Coconut

The flesh of young coconut, when it is soft and jelly-like, should be 1–3 mm thick. It can be easily scooped off the shell with a spoon. When the coconut matures, the flesh becomes thicker and harder so that it becomes more difficult to scoop off.

In the old days, they used a curved scraper, with what looked like a knuckle duster on one end, to scrape the coconut flesh into long strips.

A type of scraper that I found in Cambodia, which had been available in Penang, has a sharp, and wavy crinkle-cutter blade which can slice thicker coconut flesh. However, it is not as efficient if its profile doesn't match the curvature of the coconut shell. Look for those with a curved blade.

Slightly older coconuts are preferred by drinks-stall holders because they can get more strips from each coconut. These coconut strips are normally served with diluted coconut water, *getah anggur* (a gum resin from a tree) and *biji selasih* (basil seeds), flavoured with rose essence.

THE TENDER FLESH OF YOUNG COCONUT IS DELICIOUS BOTH IN CAKES AND TAKEN WITH ICE-COLD COCONUT WATER.

Squeezing Coconut Milk

Mee hoon thay is Penang Hokkien for the cotton bag used for packing flour. These bags were recycled and sewn into smaller bags for squeezing grated coconut to extract coconut milk.

The first squeeze of grated coconut produces concentrated coconut milk known as *santan thau* (*thau* means 'head' in Hokkien) or *pati santan*. This is much like virgin olive oil which is the first squeeze of the olive. *Pati santan* is the cream that is served with desserts like Sago Pudding and Pulut Hitam. Salt is traditionally added to the *santan* so that it will not go sour.

More *santan* can be recovered from the grated coconut by adding hot water to the squeezed grated coconut and squeezing a second and, sometimes, a third time to yield thin coconut milk. The Nonyas refer to this as *santan boey* (*boey* is 'tail' in Hokkien).

You can now buy UHT concentrated coconut milk in packets. The quality of commercial *santan* has improved tremendously over the years. When buying packet or tinned coconut milk, look for the ones with a high percentage of fat.

麵 GUTHRIES 最

THREE GUNS

BRAND
REG.

頂
上
麵
粉

WHITE WHEAT
ROLLER FLOUR

WEE HIN CHAN CO., LTD.

BEACH ST, PENANG

Kuih Kosui RICE FLOUR CAKES WITH GRATED COCONUT

Kuih Kosui is a snack made by steaming a batter of ground rice with tapioca flour or green bean flour and sugar. Lye water is added to give it a more springy texture. It is served coated with grated coconut.

There are two types of Kuih Kosui — the green pandan one and the brown one made with gula Melaka. Both are flavoured by pandan leaves but the green Kuih Kosui uses the pounded pandan leaves for colouring as well.

Kuih Kosui is probably the way Nonyas pronounce Kuih Kaswi, the name of a very similar traditional Malay cake. There is another view that Kuih Kosui steamed in cups — and indeed, my mother's recipe says, "pour into cups and steam" — is the same as the Indonesian Kue Lumpang or, spelled in the Malay way, Kuih Lompang.

Lumpang is what Indonesians call the mortar that is paired with a pestle. The kue, which is prepared in several colours like Kuih Kosui, is so called because, after steaming the batter in a cup, there is a depressions in the centre which makes it look like a mortar. In Malay, lompang means 'an empty space or void', which is another way of describing the depression in the cake.

My research finds that the batter for Kuih Lompang is thick or a dough is prepared for steaming. Likewise, many recipes for Kuih Kosui give instructions to boil the batter until it has thicken before steaming. However, I find this process very difficult to handle and, instead, undercook the batter so that it can be easily spooned into the cups in a baking tin for steaming.

You could also steam the batter in a tray and cut the resulting slab into small serving pieces. Note that if you use this method, the steaming time will be long especially if the Kuih Kosui is very thick.

Which ever way you choose, the batter must be hot, otherwise the rice flour will separate and sink, resulting in Kuih Kosui that is hard at the bottom and soft on the top!

Kuih Kosui

MAKES 20 KUIHS OF 6-CM DIAMETER

80 g rice flour
4 tbsps green bean flour
   (*lek tau hoon*)
390 ml water
100 g grated coconut
¼ tsp salt
2 pandan leaves
80 g *gula Melaka*
2 tsps lye water (*kee chooi*)

Mix the rice flour and the green bean flour in 185 ml of the water. Set aside for at least 30 minutes.

Spread the grated coconut on a tray and steam it for about 5 minutes. Cool, then sprinkle on the salt and mix it well with the coconut. Leave aside for coating the Kuih Kosui.

Boil water in a pot for steaming. Get the cup trays ready by wiping oil in the individual cups. Place the tray on a steamer.

Tie each pandan leaf into a knot. Chop up the *gula Melaka* coarsely.

Boil 185 ml of water in another pot, add the pandan leaves and the *gula Melaka*, and stir till the *gula Melaka* has dissolved. Remove and discard the pandan leaves.

Add the lye water to the rice and flour mixture and stir well. Pour this into the *gula Melaka* syrup and stir over low heat. Turn off the heat when the mixture starts to thicken. That is when dark streaks appear. Stir thoroughly.

Spoon the Kuih Kosui batter to fill each cup in the tray.

Steam the batter for about 10 minutes. It is ready when the colour changes from dull brown to a darker shiny brown and there are bubbles in the Kuih Kosui.

Remove from the steamer. Allow to cool before taking the *kuih*s out of the cups. Roll in the grated coconut. Transfer to a plate for serving, adding more grated coconut.

Coconut Candy

Coconut Candy is a common sweet in Malaysia and Singapore, especially among the Eurasians. The English has a version called Coconut Ice. The use of butter and vanilla essence in Coconut Candy suggests a Western influence. My mother made diamond-shaped Coconut Candy often, particularly for Chinese New Year. She used to colour her Coconut Candy a pinky red but also chose green and yellow. For flavourng, she would add vanilla essence, and, occasionally, cocoa. To make green candy, which is more appropriate for Muslim festivals, replace the vanilla essence with pandan paste for the colour as well as the pandan fragrance.

My mother's Coconut Candy uses coconut water and evaporated milk as well as the usual ingredients of grated coconut, sugar and butter. The ingredients are mixed up and heated over a medium fire to reduce the amount of water till the sugar in the mixture crystalizes. This is a tedious process as the mixture must be stirred continuously to ensure that it doesn't get stuck at the bottom of the pan and, worse, burnt. It is not easy to decide when the candy is ready. My mother's recipe mention dropping a small sample in cold water to test if the candy will harden. Another sign that the candy is ready is when the sugar on the sides of the pan turns brown. In one of my early attempts to make Coconut Candy, I ended up with caramelized Coconut Candy – an interesting flavour much like coconut sweets.

I have modified my mother's recipe to shorten the cooking time. I did this by reducing the water content of the ingredients by not using coconut water, and replacing evaporated milk with condensed milk.

Sweetened condensed milk is manufactured by adding sugar to the milk and condensing it to reduce the water content, thus making it keep longer in the tropical climate. It is used in the coffee shops of Malaysia and Singapore when you order your beverage with milk and sugar.

In the old days, before plastic bags, condensed milk tins were recycled as containers for take-away coffee, tea and other hot beverages from coffee shops. Many from my generation will also remember condensed milk tins being used, like the cigarette tins, as a measure for cooking rice.

Note that there is a problem in finding full cream (dairy) condensed milk in Malaysia; what is available is sweetened creamers made from palm oil without any trace of milk! You can substitute sweetened condensed milk with a mixture of two parts evaporated milk and one part sugar.

If you are using a fresh coconut, make sure that it is fresh. Shake it to find out how much water is in it; the ones with little water will not be fresh. The coconut flesh should be firm and not milky. Outside Southeast Asia, it is best to buy coconut only when you need it; they do not keep well. Use frozen grated coconut if possible; it saves the hassle of cracking and grating the coconut.

Coconut Candy

400 g white grated coconut
350 g sugar
200 ml sweetened
   condensed milk
¼ tsp salt
1 tbsp butter
⅛ tsp red food colouring
½ tsp vanilla essence

Grease a square 22-cm tray or equivalent with butter. Set aside.

Mix the grated coconut, sugar, sweetened condensed milk and salt together in a pot over a medium fire. When the mixture is well mixed, reduce the heat.

Cook the mixture for about 15 minutes on low heat, stirring continuously. Add the butter. Mix in the food colouring thoroughly, then include the vanilla essence.

The mixture is ready when it thickens and turns brown at the sides of the pan. Test by dropping a small sample in cold water. It is ready when the sample hardens.

Spread the mixture uniformly over the buttered tray but do not use excessive pressure; a rough textured surface is more interesting and gives a nice bite.

Cut the candy when it is still slightly soft using a pizza roller or a knife. (It is very difficult to cut the candy without fracturing it after it has hardened.) When the candy has hardened – and please be patient – cut along the same lines completely through the candy. The pieces can then be separated.

Leave aside to cool and store in an air-tight jar.

Kuih Koci GRATED COCONUT-CENTERED DUMPLINGS

Kuih Koci is most probably a Malay dish adopted by the Nonyas although there may be a distant Chinese origin.

I learned to make this kuih *and the finer points of wrapping it from my wife's aunt whom we call* jee chim.

A main component of Kuih Koci is the filling of grated coconut cooked in various sugars, including gula Melaka. *This filling is called* inti *in Malay. Inti is also used in other Nonya* kuihs *like Pulut Inti which is bed of gultinous rice topped with a blob of* inti.

For Kuih Koci, a ball of inti *is enclosed in a glutinous rice dough, steamed and wrapped with banana leaf into a cone shape and steamed again.*

According to traditional Nonya practice, Kuih Koci should not be served for happy occasions like weddings and birthdays but is served at sad occasions like funerals and death anniversaries. It is interesting that the Eurasians make Kuih Koci for Maundy Thursday.

There are several versions of the dough. This recipe uses some black glutinous rice to make the dough a purplish grey. More black glutinous rice will result in a dark dough. There is another version that uses white glutinous rice. Pandan leaves may be used to colour the dough green and give it a pandan flavour. I presume that the white and the black Kuih Koci are made for the sad occasions and the green ones for everyday snacks.

Like the Nonyas, the Eurasians also have white and black versions of Kuih Koci. However, their grated coconut filling is white because it doesn't use gula Melaka *or brown sugar.*

Other fillings are used in various new fusion recipes for Kuih Koci. These fillings are similar to those used in more recent versions of Ang Koo, like ground peanuts with sugar, and green beans.

Kuih Koci Santan is a related kuih *which has two small Kuih Koci enclosed in a coconut milk and ground rice dough. It is also steamed in a banana leaf wrapping.*

Kuih Koci

MAKES 45

Filling
250 g *gula Melaka*
3 pandan leaves
2 tbsps water
150 g brown sugar (*aw thng*)
400 g grated coconut
2 tsps cornflour

Dough
100 g black glutinous rice
Oil
Banana leaves★
75 gm sugar
300 ml coconut milk
500 g ground glutinous rice
160 ml water

★ *It is better to use banana leaves which are thinner. Thick leaves are more difficult to wrap with.*

Filling
Chop the *gula Melaka* into smaller pieces so that it will dissolve more quickly into a syrup.

Rinse the pandan leaves and tie them into a knot.

Heat up a sauce pan or wok. Put in the *gula Melaka* and the water. Stir till the *gula Melaka* has dissolved, then add the pandan leaves and the brown sugar. Continue stirring till you get a thick syrup. There shouldn't be any sediment if good quality *gula Melaka* is used. Sieve or pick out burnt sugar, if required.

Add the grated coconut to the syrup and mix well. Stir continuously for a few minutes till the grated coconut is well mixed with the *gula Melaka*. Mix the cornflour with 1 tablespoon of water and stir it into the filling. Keep stiring till the cornflour is transparent.

Let it cool, remove the pandan leaves, then fashion into balls about 2½ cm in diameter. You should get about 45 balls. Keep aside.

Dough
Soak the glutinous rice overnight in water.

Oil the surface of a steaming tray, and make ready to steam the Kuih Koci.

Clean the banana leaves; cut into circles of approximately 18 cm in diameter. Blanch the banana leaves and stack them up. Oil one side of the banana leaves. Set aside for wrapping the Kuih Koci.

Drain the water from the black glutinous rice and rinse with water. Grind the soaked black glutinous rice with about 100 ml of water in a food processor till very fine.

Dissolve the sugar in the coconut milk.

Sieve the ground glutinous rice into a large tray or onto a worktop and gradually mix in the coconut milk. Then mix in the ground black glutinous rice and the rest of the water gradually. You may not need to use all the water; use enough to get a consistent dough. Knead the dough and roll into a cylinder about 3 cm in diameter and cut off pieces about 2 cm wide. Roll each piece into a ball and flatten into a circle. The dough should be thinner at the edges. It helps if your hands are lightly oiled.

Place a ball of filling in the centre of the circle of dough and wrap it around the filling. Make sure that the dough completely encloses the filling. Roll the dough to make the Kueh Koci round. Place on the oiled steaming tray. Repeat with the remaining ingredients.

When the tray is full, steam the Kueh Koci in the tray for about 15 minutes.

Fold one circle of banana leaf into a semicircle of about 18 cm in diameter. Fold over one third of the semicircle on one side and fold over one third on the other side. Open up the middle part of the folded circle to form a cone and oil the inside.

Put one Kuih Koci into the cone. Fold over the opposite sides with overlapping leaves and then fold over the two adjacent sides to make a packet.

Place on the steaming tray with the cone pointing upwards. Repeat till the tray is filled. Steam the wrapped Kuih Koci for about 15 minutes.

Repeat with the remaining ingredients.

Kuih Koci can be eaten warm or at room temperature.

Ondeh Ondeh GULA MELAKA-CENTERED BALLS

Ondeh Ondeh is a Malay and Nonya dessert. It is a ball of dough with a liquid gula Melaka (palm sugar) center that squirts out delightfully at the first bite.

Traditionally, the dough is a mixture of ground glutinous rice and pandan extract. The pandan leaves are pounded, mixed with water and sieved to obtain a green juice. This is mixed with the glutinous rice flour to give Ondeh Ondeh flavour and colour.

The dough is wrapped around gula Melaka and rolled into a ball. Each Ondeh Ondeh made by the Malays, and especially the Nonyas, is small enough to be taken elegantly in one mouthful. Its other name, Kuih Buah Melaka implies that it is the size of buah Melaka (Indian gooseberry, Phyllanthus emblica) which is about 2 cm in diameter. The Nonyas will make their Ondeh Ondeh as small as possible or chomel, the Malay word for dainty.

The balls of dough enclosing gula Melaka are boiled in water and then covered in grated coconut and sesame seeds. Alas! There are no sesame seeds in the Ondeh Ondeh we buy today. It is traditional to add lye water (kee chooi) to make the dough more kwee in Hokkien or ala dente as the Italian would say. The Malays and Indonesians are more likely to use kapur (slaked lime) instead for the same purpose.

When properly made, the melted gula Melaka will burst out when you bite into the dough. There are large Ondeh Ondeh sold today but these are not likely to be made by the Malays or the Nonyas. I often wonder how people eat such large Ondeh Ondeh.

In Indonesia and in some Malaysian states, Ondeh Ondeh is a different kuih. Although it has a similar dough, the filling is different. It is also bigger — about the size of a ping pong ball — and covered in sesame seeds and deep fried. This is very similar to the Chinese dessert Jin Deui or Ma Tuan (sesame ball), suggesting that the recipe may have been brought over by the early Chinese settlers. These sesame balls have a variety of fillings — pastes made from lotus seeds, black beans, red beans and green beans; some are round and others elongated to distinguish the filling used. On the other hand, there are Chinese desserts similar to Ondeh Ondeh like Kuih Ee and other dumplings with various fillings served in syrup.

It is therefore highly probable that Ondeh Ondeh has roots in China and was adapted in Southeast Asia by the Nonyas and the locals using native ingredients.

The Ondeh Ondeh of this recipe has a significant portion of sweet potato added to the dough, thus making it a bit softer than those which uses only glutinous rice flour. The use of alkaline water is not critical and therefore optional. I do not use pandan extract to colour and flavor my Ondeh Ondeh. This is so because the orange sweet potato I use will give it colour.

Traditionally, the coconut is grated using a parut (see page 77). The kernel of the coconut is removed from the shell and any remaining shell is sliced away before grating so that the grated coconut is all white. If this is not done, the grated coconut will have specks of brown, resulting in ugly Ondeh Ondeh. It is best to steam the grated coconut so that it can be kept longer.

Ondeh Ondeh

MAKES 40

3 pandan leaves
150 ml water
1 tsp lye water
(*kee chooi*) (optional)
220 g sweet potatoes,
    orange-fleshed variety
    preferred
180 g glutinous rice

200 g white grated coconut
¼ tsp salt
1 tbsp sesame seeds
100 g *gula Melaka*

Dough
Wash the pandan leaves and tie each into a knot.

Mix the water with the lye water if using. Set aside.

Peel the sweet potatoes, cut into pieces, and keep them submerged in a pot of fresh water so that they will not discolour.

Boil the pandan leaves and the sweet potatoes in a pan of water until the sweet potatoes are soft. Use a fork to test whether the potatoes are cooked.

Drain the water and mash up the sweet potatoes.

Mix the mashed potatoes with the glutinous rice flour and then add the lye-tinted water gradually. You may not need all of the 150 ml of water for the dough. The amount depends on the type of sweet potato used as some are more moist than others.

Knead till the dough is soft and slightly sticky, although it should not be so sticky that it sticks to your hands. Add a bit more flour if the dough is too sticky or add more water if the dough is too dry.

Cover the dough or keep in a plastic bag and leave aside. It can be made ahead of time and kept in a refrigerator for a few days.

Grated Coconut and Sesame Seeds
Spread the grated coconut on a tray and steam for about 4 minutes. Allow to cool, add the salt, then mix thoroughly. Set aside for coating the Ondeh Ondeh.

Pour the sesame seeds into a saucepan over a low flame. Shake the saucepan continuously till the sesames seeds are bloated. Remove the pan from the heat just before the sesame seeds turn golden. Continue shaking the pan for a while till the saucepan has cooled down, then leave aside.

Filling

Slice the *gula Melaka* into smaller pieces. If you don't do this, the *gula Melaka*, will not melt when the Ondeh Ondeh is boiled. Form the *gula Melaka* into balls about 1 cm in diameter and set aside. Note that in cool climates, the *gula Melaka* may not stick together, so it could be slightly warmed up in a microwave oven for 10-20 seconds on medium setting.

Assembly

Knead the dough and divide into two portions. Roll each half into a long cylinder about 2 cm in diameter. Slice both into pieces of about 2 cm.

Get ready a pot of hot water for boiling the Ondeh Ondeh. Do this before rolling the Ondeh Ondeh, otherwise the dough may dry up and crack, causing the *gula Melaka* to leak out.

Take a piece of the dough, roll between the palms of your hands into a ball, then make a depression at the centre and flatten into a disc of about 3.5 cm, making the edges thinner. Place a ball of *gula Melaka* at the centre. Fold up the dough, gently stretching it to cover the *gula Melaka* to form a ball. Ensure that the edges are pressed together and sealed well, otherwise the *gula Melaka* will leak out when the Ondeh Ondeh is being boiled. Roll with the palms of both hands to refine the round shape. Place on an oiled tray so that it can be easily removed. Repeat for the remaining dough and *gula Melaka*.

Boil the Ondeh Ondeh in the prepared pot of boiling water. When they float, let them boil for at least a minute longer to allow the *gula Melaka* to melt.

Scoop out the Ondeh Ondeh with a small seive. Drain, and roll each one in the grated coconut so that it is fully coated. Repeat for the remaining Ondeh Ondeh.

Arrange the Ondeh Ondeh in a cluster. Sprinkle the toasted sesame seeds uniformly over the Ondeh Ondeh and serve when they have cooled down.

Kuih Bengka Ubi Kayu COCONUT AND TAPIOCA CAKE

Kuih Bengka Ubi Kayu, also known as Kuih Bengkang Ubi Kayu, and Kuih Bengka Beras are both Malay kuihs *adopted by the Nonyas. Kuih Bengka Beras is the plain* kuih *which is one of the assortment served at Nonya wedding receptions. The main ingredients are ground rice, sugar and coconut milk. It is off-white, but it has become more common to see Kuih Bengka coloured purple or brown. Kuih Bengka Ubi Kayu has grated tapioca as well as a small amount of grated coconut added to give it a bit of bite.*

The ingredients are mixed together and cooked before being poured into a cake tin, lined with banana leaves, for baking and grilling. Kuih Bengka is characterised by the slightly browned top.

Kuih Bengka originated from South America. Tapioca is native to Brazil and the root crop was carried to different parts of the world, including Asia and the Philippines, by Spanish and Portuguese colonizers. Bolo de Mandico, a traditional Brazilian tapioca cake made with grated tapioca, tapioca flour, coconut milk and eggs, is almost identical to Kuih Bengka.

The origin of the name Kuih Bengka, however, is more convoluted. Binka and Bibinka is the Filipino tapioca cake, made from a similar recipe as Kuih Bengka, but uses milled glutinous rice instead of ground rice. It is poured into a special claypot lined with banana leaves and baked in a charcoal oven. But Bibingka is also the general name for rice cakes in the Philippines. There is a traditional Indian 16-layer pudding from Goa that is called Bebinca which was brought to Portugal. With the Iberian union of the Portuguese and Spanish crowns between 1580 and 1640, the name to identify cakes generally could well have been introduced to Spanish Philippines.

Ubi kayu *is the Malay name for the cassava or tapioca tuber. Ubi is Malay for 'potato' while* kayu *means 'wood'. You will understand why* ubi kayu *is so called if you have come across an old tuber which grows off the root of the tapioca plant. As the* ubi kayu *grows bigger and older, the part nearer the roots are as hard as wood! Hence, when cutting up the tapioca for Kuih Bengka, it is best to discard the woody parts.*

I have read that the African cassava is poisonous due to the presence of cyanide and have to be specially processed before it can be eaten. I am told that the edible tapiocas in Southeast Asia are the ones with leaves with red stalks, but of course they need to be cooked.

This is one of the many kuihs *taught to me by* jee chim, *my wife's aunt and my mentor. She used* cupak *(see page 16) for measuring rice and a rice bowl to measure most of her other ingredients. The whole process of converting her measures to metric was more complicated since she does not normally fill her bowl to the brim! She doesn't have a recipe book; all the details are in her head.*

Jee chim *mentioned that pink-skinned tapioca should be used. Actually, the outer skin of the tapioca is brown but beneath it is a thin layer of pink.*

Since there could be a lot of wastage, you would need to buy at least one third more tapioca than the amount required in the recipe, especially if the quality of the tapioca available is not so good.

Peel away the pink skin of the tapioca and remove the grey portions, and use only the white flesh. If older tapioca is used, the thicker, woody skin close to the stalk must be removed so there won't be any hard fibres after grating. Hold the thinner end of the tapioca when grating.

It is possible to buy fresh tapioca and frozen grated tapioca in many countries outside Southeast Asia. These are readily available in Chinese and Indochinese shops in England.

Two types of traditional graters, or parut in Malay, are normally used to grate tapioca. They are the steel grater with barbs protruding from a galvanized plate and the one with short brass wires implanted on a wooden base.

Traditionally, a large brass wok is used to cook the tapioca mixture, and a wooden ladle is used as a stirrer.

This is one of the Nonya kuihs which can be conveniently prepared using a Thermomix. The chopping of the tapioca, the mixing of the ingredients, and the continuous stirring of the mixture at a constant temperature can all be done by the machine.

Kuih Bengka Ubi Kayu

Banana leaves for lining tray
Cotton string for tying
   banana leaves to the side
   of cake tin
900 g red-skinned tapioca
60 g tapioca flour
400 g sugar
450 ml concentrated
   coconut milk, keep aside
   2 tbsp for glazing
1 egg
½ tsp salt
125 g grated coconut
6 pandan leaves, rinsed and
   knotted

Blanch or heat up the banana leaves over a fire to soften them. Line a 18 x 18 cm tray with the banana leaves allowing for overhang. Fold the overhanging leaves against the outside of the tray and tie the leaves to the tray with the string to ensure that the leaves will not warp during baking.

Remove the hard, woody parts and the skin of the tapioca. Grate the tapioca. I have been advised to rest the grated tapioca for liquid to drain but, from my experience, not much liquid comes out from the tapioca I have grated.

Combine the grated tapioca, the tapioca flour, sugar, the coconut milk, egg, salt and mix thoroughly in a large wok. Then add the water and stir well. Now mix in the grated coconut.

Put the mixture over medium heat and stir continuously with a wooden stirrer. Lower the heat once the mixture is heated through.

Add the pandan leaves and continue to stir the mixture. The stirrer should be in constant contact with the surface of the wok and moved over the whole surface to ensure that the mixture is not burnt. Stir for about 20 minutes till the mixture is sticky and transparent. Remove the pandan leaves.

Transfer the mixture into the lined tray, ensuring that the corners of the tray are filled up and that there are no gaps at the edges and corners.

Use a folded banana leaf to spread 2 tablespoons of concentrated coconut milk over the mixture to glaze. At the same time, level the mixture in the tray.

Bake in an oven at 180°C for an hour. After about 40 minutes, check that the top is not burnt. Cover with foil if the top is already brown.

Remove the cake from the oven and leave it aside until cool and hardened before slicing. Cut into pieces of about 1 x 4 x 7 cm.

Cendol GREEN BEAN JELLY DESSERT

Cendol *is a short, green, worm-like jelly made from a paste of ground rice or green bean flour. The gluey mix is wiped through a sieve to form the elongated, tear-shaped* cendol.

The cendol *jellies are served with coconut milk, palm sugar and, more recently, with shaved ice. Pandan leaves colour the jellies green and give it its fragrance. Two other leaves are also used to give it a more intense green –* daun suji (Dracaena angustifolia) *and* mani chai *in Hokkien or* sayur manis *in Malay* (Sauropus androgynus). Mani chai *is used in my mother's Cendol recipe.*

My earliest recollection of Cendol was that sold by Mamak hawkers. The dessert was all mixed, ready to serve in the type of perspex container trimmed with bright colours still used to sell drinks by hawkers today. The Mamaks simply dished out a bowl when you made your order. There were rumours then that worms were added to help the Cendol keep longer. I should explain that coconut milk will go sour if kept for too long in the tropical temperature. I suspect that the rumours were propagated by our parents to discourage us from buying Cendol from these stalls.

At the higher-end stalls or in restaurants in Malaysia and Singapore, each bowl or glass of Cendol is prepared individually. Ice is shaved over the cendol *jellies and the coconut milk and palm sugar are spooned over.*

Versions of Cendol are also found throughout Southeast Asia. The Thais call it Lot Chong (translated aptly as 'gone through a hole'), the Vietnamese Bánh Lot (fall through cake), and the Cambodians, simply Lot. In Myanmar, the name is Mont Let Saung (literally 'bread winter'). In Indonesia, where the dessert is thought to have originated, it is also known as Cendol from the Javanese/Sundanese word jendol which means 'bump or bulge'.

My Facebook friend Katy Biggs suggested that the origins could go to China because of the way cendol *is made. It may have evolved from a Chinese short rice noodle brought to Indonesia by the early Chinese settlers. The noodle is called silver needle noodles in Hong Kong and Taiwan, and is also known in Mandarin as* lao shu fen *because it resembles rat droppings or tails. In Hokkien, the name is* bee tai bak *or* mee tai bak. *This noodle, like other Chinese noodles, is served in a soup or could be fried. In the old Straits Settlements, red and white* bee tai bak *were served in a syrup as a Nonya dessert; some versions were multicoloured.*

The bee *in* bee tai bak *means 'rice',* tai *means 'sieve', and* bak *means 'eye', referring to how* bee tai bak *and* cendol *noodles are made. For* bee tai bak, *ground rice is made into a dough which is wiped over a metal sheet with numerous eye holes punched through. The bits of noodles thus formed are cooked when they fall into boiling water over which the sieve is placed. For* cendol, *the dough is first cooked before being passed through a sieve to fall into a basin of ice-cold water.*

The transition from savoury bee tai bak *to the sweet Cendol in Java could be similar to the* adaptation of the mainly Hokkien dishes to Nonya dishes using local ingredients in the Straits Settlements. With Cendol, common indigenous produce like pandan leaves, coconut milk and palm sugar were employed.

I have looked at many Cendol recipes from Southeast Asia. Most of the recipes especially from Thailand, Vietnam and Cambodia, and to some extent from Indonesia, use ground rice as the main ingredient. In Malaysia, the Malays tend to also use ground rice while the Nonyas use grean bean flour. Some Indonesian recipes also use *hoon kue*, which is basicaly green bean flour. Smaller quantities of other types of flour from tapioca, sago and potato are added to alter the texture of the cendol jelly to make it more shiny and al dente. The addition of lye water or lime water enhances the green of the jelly.

In Malaysia and Indonesia, the palm sugar from the coconut tree — known as gula Melaka in Malaysia — is added to the Cendol dessert. In Java, India, Burma, Thailand, Vietnam and Cambodia the sugar from a different palm tree — Palmyra Palm (Borassus) — is commonly used.

Somewhere along the line, boiled red beans were added by the Chinese and glutinous rice by the Indians. I suspect it was to add more bulk to the dish. In more recent times, ice cream, durian, sago and sweet corn and other ingredients have been added. So what's new? Cendol jelly was put in Ice Kacang a long time ago!

The Teochew Cendol stall at Keng Kwee Street, off Penang Road, is a well-known stall in Penang. The last time I had Cendol there, I was very disappointed to notice that the cendol jelly they served didn't have the traditional shape. I suspect their jellies are no longer made with the traditional sieve but most probably a press for thick rice vermicelli. I am sure it is possible to mass produce cendol jellies in the traditional shape as I have seen factory-made bee tai bak with its proper shape.

I understand that Jeta Groves in Malacca is a good place to go to for Cendol as well as other Nonya dishes.

Cendol

450 g grated coconut
150 ml water
¼ tsp salt
150 g *gula Melaka*
50 g brown sugar
2 pandan leaves, knotted
Shaved Ice

Cendol jelly
20 pandan leaves★
850 ml water
1 tsp lye water
110 g green bean flour
   (*lek tau hoon*)
1 tbsp tapioca flour

Equipment
Cendol sieve. If a traditional
one is not available, a
colander with holes about
4 mm could be used.

You will need a spreader
with a curved edge for
forcing the *cendol* dough
through the sieve.

Prepare a container with ice
water to collect the *cendol* as
they leave the sieve.

★ Note: an equivalent
amount of *daun suji*, *mani
chai* or combination of both
could be used.

Squeeze the grated coconut to get about 220 ml of
first-squeeze coconut milk. Mix 150 ml of water
with the squeezed grated coconut and squeeze again
to get 150 ml of second-squeeze coconut milk for
mixing with the *gula Melaka*. Alternatively, use a
good quality commercial coconut milk which has
over 20 percent fat. Reserve 200 ml of the coconut
milk. Mix 20 ml of the coconut milk with 150 ml of
water to make a thin milk.

Dissolve the salt in the first-squeeze coconut milk
and leave aside for serving with the Cendol.

Boil the second-squeeze coconut milk with the
pandan leaves. Dissolve the *gula Melaka* and the
brown sugar in this. Leave aside to cool down for
serving with the Cendol.

To make the *cendol* jelly, chop up the pandan leaves
and put them in a food processor to blend. Add just
enough water, a little at a time, for the pandan leaves
to blend smoothly. Squeeze out the juice from the
blended pandan. Mix more water to the squeezed
pandan and squeeze again. Repeat for a third
squeeze. Altogether the recipe calls for 850 ml of
pandan juice. Add the lye water to the pandan juice
to enhance the colour

Combine in a pan the green bean flour, the tapioca
flour, and the pandan juice. It may be more convenient to halve the portions and do this step twice.

Put this over a low fire. Stir continuously, especially
when it begins to thicken and the colour darkens.

Put the sieve at least 15 cm above a container of
iced water to ensure that the length of each *cendol* is
not too short. Transfer the *cendol* dough to the sieve
and use the spreader to press the dough through the
sieve. Leave the jellies in the cold water and drain
only before serving.

Serve the *cendol* jellies in a bowl or glass with the
coconut milk syrup, the thick coconut mik and ice.

Coconut Water

The water and the soft, young flesh of the coconut make an excellent drink, especially if it is chilled in the refrigerator. It is best taken neat, without ice which will only dilute the coconut water. The best and sweetest water and flesh come from small, green, and naturally pandan flavoured coconuts; next in sweetness are the the small, orange or brown coconuts. The larger green coconuts, the least sweet, are the ones used for cooking.

My brother and I used to climb up coconut trees to pluck the young coconuts in our aunt's garden. We cut off the top of the coconut and drank the water straight out of the coconut. Then we chopped the coconut into two and sliced off a bit of the young husk to use as a scrapper to scoop up the tender coconut flesh.

The flesh of a young coconut should be less than ¼ cm thick, soft and jelly-like, and can be scraped off the shell easily with a spoon. When the coconut matures, the flesh becomes thicker and harder, and you will need a special scrapper to remove the flesh.

I remember coconut water served with young coconut strips in Mamak stalls in Penang. The most famous one is the Ais Tingkat stall next to the Penang Road Chowrasta Market. It is also known as Window Sherbet (or serbat in Malay) because it is sold through a window in Tamil Street.

The Mamak hawker version has rose essence added as well as getah anggur (a gum resin from a tree), and biji selasih (basil seeds) which plumps up to look like frog's eggs when soaked in water.

Extracting the Coconut Water and the Flesh
You will need a parang or a large chopper to do the job.

A simple way of extracting the coconut water is to cut off the top of the coconut where the stalk is. This is the softer part of the coconut shell. Some coconuts are sold with the husk at the top and the bottom of the coconut removed. The fatter side is the top of the coconut.

Slice off more of the husk from the top to expose the coconut shell and the three holes which looks like two eyes and a mouth. Use a chopper or a small knife to make a hole near the 'mouth' to extract the coconut water.

Once the coconut water has been drained, chop the coconut into two with a heavy stroke to the top of the coconut. You may need to chop a few times. If the chopper is stuck to the coconut, lift the coconut with the chopper and bash the coconut onto the ground.

Once the coconut is split open, use your fingers to remove the splintered shell from the coconut flesh and a tablespoon to scrape off the flesh. If the flesh is thick, you could use a lemon zester although it is not so efficient because the alignment of the holes is straight and not curved. In the old days, the lemon-zester like scrappers we had were curved.

Sesargon SUGARED DESICCATED COCONUT

We call it Sesargon (pronounced see-sar-goan). Also known as Sargon, and Sarsagon, it is one Nonya heritage tit-bit that I ate when I was young. Tit-bit is quite the right description because you could say Sesargon is a very posh version of sugared desiccated coconut. The main ingredients are grated coconut, ground rice and egg. These are mixed together and fried over low heat in a traditional brass pan with pandan leaves to give it the flavour. Sugar is the last ingredient to be added.

Traditionally, the rice is ground using a cheok bo *or stone grinder (see page 33). A true-blue nonya will use a* parut *(see page 77) to labouriously grate the coconut by hand.*

There are several recipes in old cookbooks for Sesargon but, like all vintage recipes, most are not very specific about details. My cousin Sandy told me that her mother fried the grated coconut and ground rice separately. I wanted the version in which the grated coconut and the ground rice are mixed together with a bit of egg and kapur *(slaked lime). The challenge is to uniformly coat the grated coconut bits with egg,* kapur *and ground rice without forming too many large lumps while frying. It took me nearly four hours during my first session of developing the recipe to find a better way of mixing the elements; I even tried microwaving the mixture! Finally, I discovered that it is best to fry the grated coconut first to remove some of the moisture and then mix in the other ingredients. Fine sugar is added to the fried grated coconut after it has cooled down. Store the Sesargon in air-tight bottles to keep it crispy.*

It is most probable that Sesargon has a Malay origin, since the main ingredients – both rice and coconut – are readily available in the kampongs of Malaya. The Nonyas adopted it and it is still available commercially in Malacca. My cousin Yvonne kindly brought me a bottle of Sesargoan from Malacca. I brought it to Penang for my siblings and cousins to try. Their verdict: there is too much sugar and it is too fine so you cannot taste the coconut or the rice. Sesargon is also available in some of the southern Thai towns like Phuket and Hatyai, where there is a sizable population of Babas. My sister occasionally buys me small packets of Sesargon in cylindrical plastic tubes from Hatyai. I found Sesargon packed in large paper cones when I visited Hatyai; they were about five times the size of the dainty Sesargon cones we had in Penang.

The proper way to eat Sesargon from a paper cone is to tear off the bottom, tilt your head backward and tap the cone to let the Sesargon flow out into your mouth a little at a time. A word of caution is needed here: make sure it doesn't get into your air passage!

I packed the Sesargon in cones made from A6 size paper. I had feedback saying that it was very difficult to tear the bottoms of the paper cones because the paper I used was too thick! My sister Ai and our nooi chim *told me that the thin grease-proof tracing paper used for baking was traditionally used for making Sesargon cones.*

Sesargon

800 g white grated coconut
½ tsp salt
1 egg
300 g ground rice
¼ tsp slaked lime (*kapur*)
4 pandan leaves, rinsed and
   cut into 3-cm strips
140 g sugar

Paper Cones
Grease proof paper
Glue or cello-tape

Mix the grated coconut and salt. Fry the grated coconut in a heavy pan or wok over a medium heat for about 10 minutes to remove some of the moisture so that it is easier to mix it with the other ingredients. Set aside.

Beat up the egg and spread it evenly over the grated coconut. Use your thumb and fingers to mix the egg and the grated coconut together. Sieve the ground rice uniformly over the grated coconut. Rub the slaked lime between your fingers and thumb and mix it up with all the other ingredients. A food processor with a blunt blade could be employed to do the mixing, but manual mixing is still needed.

When all the ingredients are well mixed together, transfer the mixture to a frying pan on a low fire. Initially, the mixture will be quite lumpy but as it gets drier it becomes easier to break up the lumps into smaller pieces. After about 15 minutes, add the pandan leaves and spread them among the Sesargon.

Use the frying ladle to constantly stir to continue to break up any lumps. The fire should be low, otherwise parts of the Sesargon will turn brown very quickly. The task of constantly stirring to move the Sesargon away from the surface of the pan to the top needs patience. Continue frying for at least 1½-2 hours till the Sesargon is crispy and just off-white but not quite golden.

Remove and discard the pandan leaves which would have shrank by this stage. Leave to cool, then mix in the sugar thoroughly.

Cut grease-proof tracing paper into A6-size (approx. 150 x 100 mm) sheets. Fold each sheet into a thin cone. Use glue or cello-tape to fasten the paper cone together.

Fill up each cone with about 1½-2 tablespoons of Sesargon and fold over the top to cover. Repeat till the all the Sesargon has been packed. Keep the Sesargon cones in an air-tight container.

Kitchen Utensils From Plants

Coconut palms, bamboo bushes, and banana trees are ubiquitous in the kampongs and rural areas of Malaysia, Singapore and other parts of Southeast Asia. It is therefore not surprising that there are so many products which are made from parts of these plants that are used in regional cooking, including Nonya cuisine.

COCONUT TREE

We have seen from the previous chapter that the coconut is used in many ways in the Nonya kitchen. Besides the coconut being an ingredient for cooking, other parts of the coconut tree are also used to wrap food or to make cooking utensils.

Coconut Leaves

Coconut fronds have leaflets on either side of each stalk. Young, yellowish-green leaflets are woven into square pouches which are filled with rice, and boiled to make Ketupat. The confined space within the pouch compresses the rice as it is cooked, so that when the leaves are taken apart, rice cakes are revealed. Ketupat is served with satay or put in Longtong.

In Singapore and the southern Malaysian states, two coconut leaflets of about 25 cm each are used to contain the filling for Panggang Otak (spicy fish cake); both ends of the leaves are pinned togther with a short piece of *lidi*.

Lidi (pronounced *lili* by the Penang Hokkiens) is the midrib of the coconut leaflet obtained by stripping away the leafy parts.

LIDI, THE MIDRIB OF THE COCONUT LEAFLET, BEING MADE INTO SATAY SKEWERS.

Midribs of Coconut Leaves

Satay sticks were originally *lidi* although virtually all Satay sticks today are made of bamboo. These midribs, when bunched and tied together, are still used as brooms, especially in gardens and wet areas.

When you take a *blangah* (traditional claypot) or a wok off the fire, where do you place it? In the Nonya kitchen, you place it on a pot holder, woven from lidi, designed to provide a stable base for hot cooking vessels with round bottoms. These pot holders are known as *lekar* in Malay and *bok keng loak* – literally 'putting the claypot down' – in Hokkien. *Lekar* could also be woven from sliced rattan. Both the *blangah* and *lekar* are still used in my own, my family's, and aunt's kitchens.

My mother used a *lidi* to test if her cakes were ready. She would inserted one into a cake and the *lidi* would come out clean when the cake was ready.

Just as *lidi* can be woven into baskets, and fruit trays, coconut leaves can also be used to weave mats for drying ingredients, and baskets for storing and steaming food.

Coconut Shells and Trunk

Senduk is Malay for ladle. The traditional ladle has a wooden handle connected to a scoop made from a coconut shell. The *senduk* comes in various shapes and sizes.

I have come across a large half coconut shell used as a pail for bathing.

The hard wood from the outer part of coconut trunks is used to make utensils like handles for *senduk*, plates, serving forks and spoons, chopsticks and chopstick holders.

BAMBOO
Bamboo (*Bambusoideae*) is a member of the grass family that grows all over East and Southeast Asia. It is one of the fastest-growing plants and, as such, bamboo products are more environmentally sustainable than other wood products.

The stem and leaves of the bamboo have a wide variety of uses in the kitchen.

Bamboo Steamers

Steaming is an important way of cooking in China and in Southeast Asia. Nonya cooks use Chinese bamboo steaming trays which come in all sizes, although they rarely use the small steaming trays for cooking and serving *dim sum*. I use a large steamer for steaming glutinous rice for Pulut Taitai, Nasi Lemak, and many *kuih*s like Kuih Lapis, Kuih Kosui and Kuih Koci.

The Thais have a steaming basket for steaming glutinous rice without the need for any lining. It looks like an overturned hat, and I understand it is in fact used as a hat during the Thai Water Festival. It goes with a pot with a wide, flared rim designed to support the basket. I have used them for steaming Nasi Kunyit.

Sieve

I remember the Indian Mee Rebus and Mee Goreng man using a sieve with a bamboo basket and bamboo handle for blanching noodles and beansprouts. Today, the basket is made from brass wire but the handle remains bamboo. The Wantan Mee man uses a shallower version of this type of sieve for blanching the noodles.

Colanders and Trays

Bamboo is used to make colanders of various shapes and sizes. Larger trays are also made from bamboo. They are called *karlow* in Hokkien and *nyiru* in Malay respectively. The *nyiru* is used for winnowing rice and for drying all types of food stuff such as dried prawns, salt fish, *keropok* and Lem Peng, a near extinct crispy Nonya Chinese New Year goodie made from rice.

Chopsticks

Chopsticks were largely made from bamboo before plastic came along. Today's generation is more familiar with disposable ones which can also be made of bamboo.

Bamboo Skewers

In the culinary world, bamboo is used to fashion skewers of all shapes, sizes and thickness. Most of today's Satay sticks are made of bamboo.

Bamboo Knocker

For those old enough to remember, the old mobile Wantan Mee hawker hit a large piece of bamboo with a small stick to make the rhythmic tick-tock sound which announced his arrival.

Bamboo Leaves

Traditional Bak Chang or rice dumplings can be wrapped in dried bamboo leaves. To prepare them for use, the leaves are soaked in water to soften them.

BANANA TREE

The banana tree is a large, tropical herbaceous flowering plant in the genus *Musa*. The fruit is botanically considered a berry. Banana plants are fast-growing perennials which replace themselves from rhizomes. The leaves are long, broad and graceful while the trunk is made up of layers of leaf sheaths.

Banana Leaves

Banana leaves, being inexpensive, waxy and yet pliable, are traditionally used to wrap a whole range of raw or cooked food. In the past, when we bought *rempah* in the market, it would be wrapped in banana leaves. Likewise, cooked food like Nasi Lemak and Pulut Inti were bundled in banana leaves.

A very large number of *kuih*s are wrapped in banana leaves for steaming. These include the savoury Rempah Udang, and the sweet Lepat Pisang, Kuih Koci Santan, and Kuih Bongkong.

Like Kuih Koci Santan, and Kuih Bongkong, the Northern Nonya version of Otak-Otak is enclosed in banana leaves pinned together with a short *lidi*. Banana leaves are also used to encase marinated fish for grilling. Ikan Panggang is a classic dish which uses this technique. The best banana leaves to wrap food for cooking are from Pisang Batu and Pisang Rajah as their leaves are thin and soft so that there is no need to blanch them before use.

Banana leaves are commonly used by the Southern Indians for serving food. By custom, the leaves are folded away from the diner after the meal.

Bananas leaves were widely used to wrap takeaway food. In Penang, Yee Foo Mee, Ho Fun and Char Kway Teow were wrapped in newspaper lined with bananas leaves. Similarly, our local fruit *rojak* man at Pulau Tikus sold *rojak* in a cone of old newspaper lined with a piece of banana leaf pinned in place with a short length of *lidi*.

Some say that the banana leaves impart a flavor to hot food wrapped in it. That is why Char Koay Teow today is served with a token piece of banana leaf in some stalls in Penang.

THE TYPE OF BAMBOO KNOCKER USED BY THE WANTAN MEE HAWKERS TO ANNOUNCE THEIR PRESENCE.

Unfortunately, the environmentally friendly banana leaves have been virtually replaced today by plastic and grease-proof paper.

Banana Trunk

The trunk of the banana plant is not a real tree trunk but a pseudostem. It is made up of multiple layers which are actually the extension of the banana leaf stalks.

The banana tree dies after the bananas have been harvested. In the old days, when the tree trunks were chopped down, they were not wasted; they were chopped up, cooked with other food waste, and fed to pigs.

The fibre of banana trunks were also made into strings – used by the Chinese as well as the Indians. I still see such strings used for tying flower garlands in Little India in Singapore.

After being dried and treated, the leaf stalks are today plaited into household products like trays, tablemats and used to decorate photo frames.

I have made my own banana strings by first separating the leaf stalk, piece by piece. I then cut each stalk about 1 cm wide along the length according to the grain of the fibre. So, the strings can be as long as the tree trunk. The strings are ready to be used after being dried in the sun.

OTHER LEAVES AND GRASSES

Although banana and bamboo leaves are still used today for wrapping food, the leaves of several other plants are not so commonly used today. These include pandan, *opeh*, lotus, Simpoh Air and various palm trees, besides coconut.

Pandan Leaves

There are two types of pandan – the larger, thorny *Pandanus tectorius* and the small *Pandanus amaryllifolius*. Both are commnly known as screwpine.

The leaves of the former were commonly used in Singapore to wrap Nonya *chang* while the small species is still used to wrap savoury foods such as Malay Otak and Thai Pandan Chicken. The small leaves are employed as a flavouring agent and green food colouring for various *kuih*.

The delicate scent of pandan has been described as rose-like and milky sweet. Some say that it has an almondy and vanilla quality.

Simpoh Air

The distinctive Simpoh Air tree (*Dillenia Suffruticosa*) has large leaves and showy yellow flowers. Almost every flower turns into a fruit with thick, red sepals, often mistaken for the flower.

In the past, especially in Singapore, Simpoh Air leaves were used for wrapping food such as Chee Cheong Fun, *rojak* and even raw meat. The leaves are still used today to wrap *tempeh*, fermented soya beans.

Lotus Leaves

The best known use for lotus leaves is for wrapping Lor Mai Kai, chicken cooked with glutinous rice. They are also used to wrap steamed rice dishes in restaurants as lotus leaves have medicinal qualities and impart a distinctive flavor to food.

Opeh

Opeh comes from the leaf sheath of the areca or *pinang* palm. It is from the inside of the sheath, closer to the tree trunk. It has fine corrugation yet has good tensile strength. Hence it is useful for wrapping food.

The leaf sheath has a paper-thin layer. I have tried to remove this, but it is not easy!

I remember *dodol* – a toffee-like confectionery made from coconut milk, coconut sugar and ground rice – being wrapped in *opeh*. Today, you will hardly find *dodol* wrapped in it as *opeh* has been replaced by plastic.

Opeh was once commonly used in Singapore to wrap takeaway food like Char Kway Teow, Fried Hokkien Mee, Carrot Cake and Chui Kueh, the *opeh* imparting a woody fragrance to the wrapped food, enhancing its flavour. Because of this, there has been a revival in the use of *opeh* as a wrapping.

I have come across very attractive disposable plates and bowls of various sizes made from *opeh*. This is a very innovative idea as these excellent products are biodegradable.

Palm Trees other than Coconut

The young leaves of the fan palm tree (*Licuala*) is used to make the triangular Ketupat Palas which is filled with glutinous rice. The leaf from the *Livistona chinensis* palm is dried and made into fans which are iconic in kitchens with charcoal stoves. They are used to fan a fire for steamboat, grilling Satay, and baking Kuih Bahulu or Kuih Kapit.

Corn Husks

Corn husks are the dried covering of corn or maize. The husk that covers each ear of maize is made up of many thin and separate layers.

In Indonesia, corn husk is used to wrap *dodol*, especially in Bali. In the Philippines, corn husk is used to wrap Tamales, a sort of dumpling of dough encasing meat or other ingredients.

Marsh Grass

Kiam chow, literally 'salty grass' in Hokkien, is an organic string made from a long-stemmed saltwater marsh grass. To make them strong and supple, the dried reeds are soaked in water before use. *Kiam chow* was commonly used to tie packages in markets, and is still used to tie wrapped rice dumplings.

CHANG, OR RICE DUMPLINGS, TIED WITH MARSH GRASS.

Satay

Satay and Sate are Southeast Asian generic names for marinated meat which has been thinly sliced, skewered and grilled over a charcoal fire. It is a popular hawker food in Malaysia, Indonesia, Singapore, Brunei, and Thailand which most probably evolved into what it is today in Java, where there is a wide variety of Satay as well as the accompanying dipping sauces. Its origins go further to India and most probably back to the Arabs in the Middle East. Close relatives of Satay are Shish Kebab from Turkey, and Yakitori from Japan.

Indonesian Satay tends to be sweeter due to the use of kecap manis *(sweet sauce). In Malaysia and Singapore, it is traditionally served with a peanut-based dipping sauce, together with* ketupat, *sliced cucumber and cut onions. Ketupat is compressed cooked rice made by weaving young, yellow coconut leaves into small pillows, filling them with rice and boiling in water. The rice is compressed within the leaves when cooked. I made my own* ketupat *in London by using freezer-to-boiler plastic bags in the days when Asian products were not readily available there.*

The halal *versions of Satay use beef, mutton and chicken. However, the Chinese who are non-Muslims also use pork. The Nonyas in Singapore serve it with a pineapple sauce or grated pineapple added to the peanut sauce. The Hainanese Satay described in my first book,* Penang Heritage Food, *is served with a sweet potato-based dipping sauce, together with toasted bread as a condiment. Traditionally, each stick of Hainanese Satay consists of two larger pieces of sliced lean meat with a thin strip of fat sandwiched in between – altogether three pieces – literally transliterated as* sah teh *in Hokkien. This is as good an explanation as any for the name of this famous dish.*

Traditionally, the skewers or Satay sticks were the midribs of the coconut leaflets – called lidi *in Malay or* lili *by the Penang Hokkiens. In more recent times,* lidis *have been replaced by imported bamboo skewers. The younger generation would not know what a* lidi *is let alone know what it looks like (see page 109).*

Satay is served in coffee shops, hawker stalls in hawker centres and on road-sides. It is commonly served in pasar malam *(night markets) in Malaysia. Nowadays, Satay is also served in restaurants and by Southeast Asian airlines to their business- and first-class passengers.*

In the old days, you did not have to decide how many sticks of Satay to order. You find a table and the Satay will be brought to you. You eat whatever you want or can and, the satay will be replenished when the supply on the table runs low. At the end, the depleted Satay sticks were counted and the charge computed. That may explain how some of my cousins consumed more than fifty sticks of Satay each in one sitting!

I remember from my youth that there were pieces of onions in the Satay sauce. I checked my late mother's recipe and found that cut onions were indeed included in the sauce. Fortunately, Satay is still served with freshly cut onions.

Satay

Ketupat
Plastic bags suitable for boiling
400 g rice

1 kg meat, cut into pieces about ½ x 1½ x 2½ cm

Marinade
2 stalks lemongrass
2 tbsps ground coriander seeds (*ketumbar*)
1 tsp ground cumin (*jintan puteh*)
1 tsp ground fennel (*jintan manis*)
1 tbsp ground tumeric (*kunyit*)
1 tsp salt
4 tbsps sugar
120 ml coconut milk
Satay sticks, soaked in water for at least one hour before use

Basting Mixture
Marinade left over from skewering
2 tbsps oil
50 ml coconut milk
1 stalk lemongrass

Ketupat
Prepare five plastic bags of about 9 x 9 cm which are suitable for boiling. You will need a plastic sealer.

Fill each bag with 80 g of raw rice and seal the bag. Perforate the bags with a thick pin or needle so that water can flow through the bags.

Place the bags of rice in a pot of water. Rinse and drain the water. Refill with enough water to completely cover the bags.

Bring to a boil and let the rice simmer for about ½ hour till cooked. Cool, drain the water from the pot, and set the *ketupat* aside.

Marinade
Cut off the roots of the lemongrass and trim away the leaves, leaving 5 cm of the white root ends. Grate the root-ends finely.

Mix the grated lemongrass and the ground spices together with the salt and sugar. Then add the coconut milk and mix well.

Add the sliced meat to the marinade, mix thoroughly, and leave aside for four hours. Keep the meat overnight in the refrigerator if necessary.

Threading Satay
Soak the Satay sticks in water so that they will not burn when the Satay is being grilled. Thread three pieces of meat one at a time on a Satay stick ensuring that the stick is not exposed between adjacent pieces of meat. This is to ensure that the stick will not burn and break while grilling.

Repeat for the remaining meat and sticks and keep aside.

Satay Sauce

300 g peanuts

2 tbsps tamarind paste,
  soaked in 100 ml water
  OR 1 tbsp vinegar

3 stalks lemongrass

3 cm diameter x 2 cm
  galangal (*lengkuas*)

5 cloves garlic

150 g shallots

6 candlenuts (*buah keras*)

2 tbsps ground coriander
  (*ketumbar*)

1½ tsps ground cumin
  (*jintan puteh*)

1½ tsps ground fennel
  (*jintan manis*)

2 tbsps chilli powder

6 tbsps oil

5 cloves

5 cm cinnamon stick

2 medium-sized onions,
each
  cut into 16 parts

1 tsp salt

6 tbsps sugar

1 litre water

100 ml coconut milk or
  milk

Condiments

2 medium-sized onions, cut
  into 12 pieces

1 cucumber, cut into
  bite-sized wedges

4 ketupats, cut into
  bite-sized pieces

Satay Sauce

It is convenient to use raw peanuts with the skins already removed. Otherwise, rub the peanuts with your fingers to remove the skins and, if you have a garden, take the tray outside and blow the skins away. An even more convenient alternative is to buy toasted peanuts! Alternatively, fry the peanuts in a wok or toast in an oven or grill till golden brown. Stir regularly so that the nuts are evenly cooked without getting burnt.

Pound half the peanuts finely and the other half coarsely so that the sauce will have a bit of crunch. This task can be quite conveniently carried out if you have a large *lesong* (mortar and pestle). A food processor can grind the nuts finely but cannot produce coarse bits in a uniform size. Combine the pounded peanuts and keep aside.

Break up the tamarind paste into small pieces and soak in 100 ml of water for at least 15 minutes. Squeeze the tamarind between your fingers and pass it through a sieve to separate the liquid from the fibre. Discard the fibre and set the tamarind liquid aside.

Cut off the root of the lemongrass and trim away the leaves, leaving 5 cm of the white root-end. Wash the galangal and cut it into smaller pieces. Smash, peel, wash and cut the garlic into quarters. Peel the shallots, wash and cut into two. Smash the candlenuts. Pound these ingredients together in a *lesong* till fine. Alternatively, grind them together in a food processor, adding 2 or 3 tablespoons of water, as required, to ensure that the ingredients are ground uniformly and finely. Add the ground spices, mix together and set this spice paste aside.

Heat up a wok and add the oil when it is hot. Fry the spice paste over medium heat. After about two minutes, add the cloves and cinnamon stick. Continue frying till fragrant and when you see the oil separating. This will take at least another 10 minutes. Add a few tablespoons of water if the spice paste becomes too dry.

Include the pounded groundnuts, the tamarind

liquid, the cut onions, the salt, sugar and half the water. Stir and bring to a boil. Simmer until the onions are transparent, adding the rest of the water when the sauce thickens. Bring to a boil again and then turn down the heat. Stir in the coconut milk and simmer till the sauce thickens again.

Grilling Satay

Mix the leftover marinade with 2 tablespoons of oil and the coconut milk to make a basting mixture for grilling the Satay.

It is best to grill Satay over charcoal embers. A fan would be useful to stoke the fire to char the Satay slightly. Alternatively, an electric or gas grill could be used.

Baste the Satay with the basting mixture while cooking. Return to tradition by using a stalk of lemongrass for basting. Trim off the top of the leaves and the hard stalk near the root, leaving a stalk about 12 cm long. Smash the root-end with a chopper to spread it out and to soften the end for use as a brush.

Serve the grilled Satay with the Satay sauce and the condiments of onions, cucumber and Ketupat.

Nasi Kunyit TUMERIC RICE

Nasi Kunyit is a traditional Malay dish. Nasi *is 'rice' in Malay, while* kunyit *means 'yellow'.* Kunyit *is also the Malay name for the orangey-yellow ginger or tumeric. Glutinous rice is soaked in water with fresh pounded or ground tumeric to give the dish its characteristic yellow colour. It is cooked with coconut milk to give it a* lemak *or creamy texture, and whole peppercorns are added to give the rice a slight peppery flavour. The peppercorns are not meant to be eaten unless you like its piquant taste. Nasi Kunyit is served with Gulai Ayam (chicken curry) or lamb curry.*

Nasi Kunyit is associated with babies' first month celebrations in Baba culture. Carried in a siah nah *(bamboo basket), it is distributed with chicken curry and Ang Koo Kuih to friends and relatives. The rice is a wish for the baby to always have a staple meal, the chicken, that there will be meat regularly on the table.*

Nasi Kunyit with curry is also used as offerings to nyatoks *— local land guardian spirits. My jee kor (second aunt) and Aunt Rosie lived away from Penang. Whenever they returned to Penang they would pai nyatoh or make prayer offerings to the nyatok. They would go to their old kampong at Tanjong Tokong where they grew up, and ask one of their ex-neighbours to prepare Nasi Kunyit and chicken curry. The dishes were taken to the seaside of Tanjong Tokong and offered to the nyatok. For a long time, I wondered why they did not cook the dishes themselves as they were very capable cooks. Then it dawned on me that the offerings must be halal — prepared and cooked in the proper Muslim way.*

Glutinous rice is used to cook Nasi Kunyit. As it takes longer to cook polished rice than glutinous rice, too much polished rice mixed up with the glutinous rice will make the Nasi Kunyit gritty because of the uncooked rice. In the past, the whole family would be involved in separating the polished rice from the glutinous rice the day before Nasi Kunyit was cooked. The rice was spread out on a large tray or dulang *in Malay and Penang Hokkien dialect, and we would sit around it to meticulously pick through the rice. The dulang is about 60 centimetres in diameter. There are brass ones, wooden ones and enameled ones with floral designs.*

Various steamers can be used for steaming Nasi Kunyit. Traditionally, the Nonyas use a bamboo steamer lined with banana leaves to prevent the rice from falling between the bamboo slats. In London, we use J-cloth instead. Daiso sells a steaming cloth which I find useful. You can also use a circular stainless-steel tray which can fit in a wok. The Thais have a conical, hat-like bamboo steamer placed over a bulbous pot. (Steamed glutinous rice is an important part of the Northern Thai diet.) It is a very convenient steamer to use since there are no large gaps and there is no need to line the steamer. Nowadays, there are various steaming pots available, including electric ones.

Nasi Kunyit

6 cm turmeric root
  OR 1 tbsp ground
  tumeric (*kunyit*)
1 coconut, grated
  OR 220 ml thick coconut
  milk
1 tsp salt
1 large calamansi lime
  (*limau kesturi*)
500 g glutinous rice
½ tbsp whole peppercorns
6 pandan leaves

If using fresh turmeric, remove the skin, chop up the turmeric and pound or grind in a food processor till fine. Mix with the water to be used for soaking the glutinous rice. Pour the water through a fine sieve and discard the sediment. Wash the glutinous rice and soak it in the turmeric water overnight or for at least 6 hours.

If using ground turmeric, wash the glutinous rice and mix well with the ground tumeric. Use enough water to cover the rice and soak overnight or for at least 6 hours.

If using grated coconut, squeeze out the thick coconut milk using a piece of muslin and add the salt to it. Set aside.

Slice the lime into two, remove the seeds and squeeze out the juice. Keep aside.

Place a steamer in a wok. Line the steamer with muslin or J-cloth.

Drain the rice and put it in the steamer. Pour about 2 litres of boiling water all over the rice; the hot water will drain into the wok to allow for steaming. Mix the peppercorns followed by the lime juice into the rice. Spread the rice out in the steamer and place the pandan leaves over the rice. Cover the steamer. Heat the water in the wok till boiling, and steam the rice for about 15 minutes.

Sprinkle the thick coconut milk over the rice and stir well to mix evenly. Cover and steam for a further 5 minutes. Stir to turn over the rice and steam for another 5 minutes till the rice is cooked.

Serve with lamb or chicken curry.

Lamb or Chicken Curry

This meat curry has strong a Indian influence; it uses Indian seed spices like coriander, cumin, fennel and cardamon. Chicken or lamb can be used. It is an early Indian-Malay fusion food which is cooked by the Nonyas as well as the Malays. This type of curry is traditionally served with Nasi Kunyit or Roti Chennai or with plain rice and other dishes.

Traditionally, the seed spices are fried or toasted before being ground individually using the batu giling. *The rest of the spice paste or* rempah *is also ground with the* batu giling *which achieves a very fine paste.*

Coconut oil is traditionally used by the Nonyas and Malays for cooking curries. My mother used to make her own virgin coconut oil by slowly heating up coconut milk to separate the very fragrant oil, and leaving behind a crispy crust.

Lemongrass, instead of curry leaves, is added to give the curry a distinct flavour.

Lamb or Chicken Curry

1 kg meat, lamb or chicken
600 g potatoes
250 g tomatoes, about
    4 medium-sized ones

Spice Paste
4 cm old ginger
2 cloves garlic
200 g shallots
150 ml water
3 tbsps chilli powder
    OR 25 g dried chilli
4 tbsps coriander powder
4 tsps cumin powder
4 tsps fennel powder
1 tsp tumeric powder
    OR 20 g fresh tumeric

½ cup oil, preferably
    coconut oil

Whole Spices
2 star anise
6 cm cinnamon stick
4 cloves
5 cardamoms, crushed
5 stalks lemongrass, use only
    the white root ends,
    crushed

150 ml coconut milk
1 tsp salt or to taste

Cut up the lamb into 2-cm cubes and set aside, or cut the chicken into serving pieces and set aside.

Peel the potatoes and cut into 2½–cm cubes. Soak in water and set aside. Cut the tomatoes into quarters and set aside.

Scrape off the skin of the ginger with the blunt side of a knife and slice the ginger finely. Set aside.

Smash the garlic, remove the skin and chop the garlic finely. Peel the shallots, wash and slice into half or quarters.

Grind the garlic and the shallots in a food processor, then add the ground spices and 150 ml of water, blending into a fine paste.

Heat up a wok or *blangah*. Add the oil and gently pour in the spice paste and stir on low to medium heat for 10 minutes.

Then add the sliced ginger, the star anise, the cinnamon, cloves, cardamom and the crushed lemongrass. Continue to *tumis* (sauté) until the oil separates from the spice paste and it darkens in colour. This could take about another 15-20 minutes. Add a tablespoon of water if the spice paste is too dry and sticks to the wok.

Add 50 ml of the coconut milk, 500 ml of water and the meat. Stir well, and bring to the boil. Then add the potatoes and bring to the boil again. Add the tomatoes and then simmer for about 20 minutes till the meat is soft. Allow to cool. You can keep the curry at this state overnight in the fridge.

To finish the curry, add another 200 ml of hot water, the remaining coconut milk and the salt. Mix thoroughly and heat it up on low to medium heat, stirring occasionally. When it has boiled, reduce the heat and simmer for a few minutes.

Serve with rice, Nasi Kunyit, Roti Jala or Roti Chennai.

Wantan Mee WONTON NOODLES

Wantan Mee is a thin, wheat-flour-based egg noodle of Cantonese origin. In Malaysia and Singapore, Wantan Mee is a popular hawker food. Mee is the Hokkien word for noodles, while the Cantonese say meen. *Wantan, pronounced* wuntun *in Cantonese, is a made by wrapping a filling in a skin made from a dough similar to the noodle; it is rolled into thin sheets and cut into squares. The filling consists mainly of prawns and meat, both coarsely minced. Traditionally, pork is used but other meats could be employed. The wantan is normally boiled but the deep-fried version is sometimes offered.*

How good Wantan Mee is, is judged by its noodles. In the old days, the noodles were handmade using only flour, duck eggs and no water, but lye water was added to make the noodles springy. It is claimed that a strand of such noodles will burn if lit while a noodle made with water will not. Today, chicken eggs are used instead of duck eggs. The noodles were traditionally made by pressing the dough with a thick bamboo pole before being cut into strands. Now, it is all done by machines similar to an Italian pasta maker. Wantan skins were similarly made and were so thin that the meat filling could be seen through the skin when cooked. The perfect wantan *should be soft and smooth, living up to its name which means 'swallowing clouds'. To achieve this,* wantans *in Hong Kong are placed in the bowl of soup below the noodles.*

The quality of the noodles and the way they are prepared also make the difference between a good and mediocre bowl of Wantan Mee. The Hong Kong variety of noodles is preferred because they are more khew *(in Hokkien) or al dente. The noodles should be blanched in boiling water and then cooled in cold, running tap water using a* hiah *(a wired sieve). The noodles are then drained before being quickly plunged in boiling water again.*

I grew up observing the Wantan Mee man doing all this unlike my daughter who did not have such exposure. The first Wantan Mee she served in her university days was a lump of noodles in soup. The Wantan Mee man loosens the skein of noodles before blanching it, and he blanches one skein at a time. Besides that, the water for blanching must be boiling hot; there must be a large enough volume of water so that the temperature does not drop significantly when he adds the noodles. And he changes the boiling water when it becomes cloudy.

This dish can be ordered as a soup version. I understand that the dry version (kon lo), which is served with the wantan *in a separate bowl of soup, is a more recent innovation.* Wantan *can also be ordered separately, served in a bowl of soup with vegetables.*

The soupy version of Wantan Mee is topped with wantan, *blanched* chai sim *(mustard greens) and sliced* char siu *(grilled meat). The original Wantan Mee of Hong Kong and*

THE AUTHOR AT THE HUMOROUS STREET ART IN CHINA STREET, PENANG, WHICH SHOWS THE WANTAN MEE HAWKER'S ASSISTANT CALLING THEIR WARES WITH A BAMBOO TOK TOK KNOCKER.

Guangzhou was not served with char siu. In Singapore and Malaysia, it is traditionally accompanied by sliced pickled green chillies in light soya sauce.

Like many soup dishes, the stock is very important. Traditionally, pork bones, dried flat fish, and/or soya beans were boiled in water and simmered for a good stock. Dried flat fish has been replaced with the cheaper ikan bilis (anchovies), although ikan bilis is now becoming too expensive to use for stocks – an effect of selective inflation on food! Prawn shells can also be used. If making your own stock is too much of a bother, you could use stock cubes. Nowadays there are ikan bilis, vegetable, chicken and other types of stock cubes on the market.

The noodles for the dry version of Wantan Mee is mixed with dark soya sauce and sesame oil. In Singapore, tomato and/or chilli sauce would also be added. The garnishes are finely sliced spring onions and bak eu phok (fried pork fat). An upmarket version uses a dark sauce with sliced Chinese mushrooms and optional diced chicken.

Wantan Mee is also known as Tok Tok Mee, bringing us back to the days when the street hawkers offering this dish announced their presence by hitting a slab of bamboo with a bamboo stick.

I remember that Wantan Mee was served in octagonal bowls. These bowls have different designs; the cockerel motif is the one which most people will remember because bowls of that design are still available today. A Wantan Mee stall would use octagonal bowls with a vegetable design while a Hokkien Mee stall would use the cockerel design. What intrigues me is why bowls would be made with eight sides since it is easier to make round bowls.

Wantan Mee

SERVES 12

Pickled Chillies
1 tsp sugar
¼ tsp salt
100 ml vinegar
6 green chillies

Stock
150 g soya beans
3 litres water
500 g pork or chicken bones

Wantan
1 wood ear mushroom,
    soaked in water
120 g minced pork or chicken
150 g prawns, deveined and
    chopped coarsely
5 sprigs spring onions,
    chopped
2 tsps light soya sauce
1 tsp sesame oil
Ground pepper
1 tsp cornflour or tapioca
    flour
About 50 *wantan* skins

Sauce
12 dried Chinese mushrooms,
    soaked in water
150 g chicken, de-boned
Ground pepper
½ tsp sugar
1 tbsp light soya sauce
1 tbsp oil
2 shallots, thinly sliced
5 tbsps dark soya sauce
250 ml stock
1 tbsp cornflour mixed in
    3 tbsps water
3 tbsps sesame oil

Pickled Chillies
Put the sugar, salt and vinegar in a glass bottle. Slice the green chillies and shake off as much of the seeds as possible. Blanch the chllies in boiling water, drain and transfer into the bottle of the vinegar mixture. It is best to eat the chillies when they are still crunchy.

Stock
Soak the soya beans for about 4 hours. Discard the water and rinse with fresh water. Boil 3 litres of water in a pot and add the bones. When it starts to boil again, add the soya beans. When the stock has boiled, reduce the heat and let it simmer for 3 hours.

Wantan
Cut the soaked wood ear mushrooms into very thin slices about 1 cm long. Mix them together with the minced meat, chopped prawns, spring onions, soya sauce, sesame oil, ground pepper and cornflour.

Place a *wantan* skin with a corner facing upward on a worktop and put about 1 teaspoon of filling in the middle of the skin. Wet the edges of the skin with your finger dipped in water and fold the *wantan* skin downward over the filling to make a triangle. Press the edges to seal. Bring the left edge over the right edge of the skin together and seal to make a shape like a Chinese gold ingot. Repeat for the rest of the *wantan* skins and filling. Keep aside.

Sauce
Cut off and discard the stems of the mushrooms. Slice the caps into pieces about 2-3 mm thick.

Cut the de-boned chicken into slices about 4 mm thick and 3 cm long. Marinate the sliced chicken with the ground pepper, sugar and light soya sauce.

Heat up a wok and add the oil. Put in the sliced shallots and fry for a minute. Then add the marinated

6 stalks mustard greens
  (*chai sim*), cut into 3-cm
  lengths
12 skeins *wantan* noodles
200 g Chinese barbecued
  pork (*char siew*)
  (see page 136)
6 stalks spring onions, finely
  chopped

chicken and stir continuously till the chicken meat is cooked. Include the dark soya sauce and the 250 ml of stock and bring to a boil.

Stir the cornflour mixture and pour it into the sauce, stirring continuously. When the sauce has thickened, stir in the sesame oil and turn off the fire. Set aside.

Vegetables, wantans and noodles
Blanch the mustard greens in a pot of boiling water and rinse them in cold, running water. Set aside.

Use the same water to boil the *wantans*. Do it in batches so that the water temperature does not drop significantly. Boil each batch for about one to two minutes, stirring to prevent the *wantans* from sticking to the bottom of the pot. The *wantans* are ready when the skins become translucent. Remove the wantans from the boiling water with a sieve and rinse in cold water. Set the *wantans* aside.

Replace the water in the pot if it is too cloudy, and bring to a boil. It is better to blanch only one skein of noodles at a time. The noodles must be loosened so that the strands are not entangled when they are being boiled. Once the noodles become shiny, remove them from the boiling water with a seive and rinse in a generous amount of cold water. Return the noodles into the boiling water for a short while. Repeat for the rest of the noodles.

Assembly
Place one portion of the blanched noodles in a bowl and top up with the soup. Add some mustard greens, a few *wantans*, and slices of *char siew* on top. You could add about ¼ teaspoon of the black sauce which is normally reserved for the dry Wantan Mee. Add a teaspoon of the chopped spring onions.

For the dry version, put the noodles in a bowl or on a plate. Add the mustard greens and the *char siew* on top. Spoon on about 2 tablespoons of the chicken sauce. The *wantan* and sometimes the vegetables are served separately with the soup in a smaller bowl. Add the chopped spring onions to noodles and soup.

Char Siew BARBECUED MEAT

Char siew *is Cantonese for 'barbecued meat'. It is traditionally served with roasted duck and a Chinese-style sausage with rice. Traditionally, pork is used but in Malaysia and Indonesia, the Muslims use chicken instead. The meat is coated in a marinade and grilled in an oven.*

Char siew is traditionally served in Wantan Mee. It is also used in the filling for Char Siew Pau (dumpling).

500 g pork shoulder or
  chicken breast

Marinade
2 shallots, finely chopped
1 tbsp grated ginger
1 tbsp salted soya beans,
  crushed
1 tsp salt
3 tbsps sugar
1 tbsp vegetable oil
3 tbsps light soya sauce
1 tbsp Chinese wine or
  Sherry
6 tbsps honey

Glaze
2 tbsp honey

Cut the meat into long strips about 2 cm thick. Rinse the meat and pat dry with kitchen towels.

Mix the ingredients for the marinade in a saucepan. Cook over low heat to blend the ingredients together.

Pour the marinade over the strips of meat and make sure that the meat is well coated. Place the meat in a plastic bag or a sealed container to marinate for about 4 hours or overnight in a refrigerator. If kept under refrigeration, allow time for the meat to come to room temperature before cooking.

Pre-heat an oven to 230°C. Spread the strips of meat on a rack over a baking tray lined with aluminium foil. Pat the meat dry with paper towels.

Roast in the oven for about 15 minutes. Turn over the meat and roast for another 15 minutes.

Take out the meat and glaze each piece with the honey using a brush. Return to the oven for about 2 to 3 minutes, depending on the thickness of the meat. Turn over the meat, glaze again and return to oven to roast for about 2 minutes.

Remove the meat from the oven and allow to cool before serving. Cut into thin slices to serve.

Bak Chang DRAGON BOAT DUMPLINGS

The fifth day of the fifth month of the Chinese lunar calendar is the day when the Chinese eat chang *or rice dumplings to commemorate Qu Yuan's legend. Qu Yuan, a poet and minister of the kingdom of Chu drowned himself in the Miluo River because he felt that his beloved kingdom was in such a parlous state. According to the legend, rice dumplings were thrown into the river from dragon boats to prevent fish from eating his body. Today, rice dumplings are available and eaten all the year round.*

Bak Chang are made by wrapping glutinous rice filled with various ingredients in bamboo leaves or the leaves of the giant pandanus and tied with kiam chow, *a marsh grass. It is cooked by mostly boiling in water, and sometimes steaming, for several hours.*

*There are many varieties of these dumplings. Each Chinese dialect group has its own variation. The Hokkien version is called Kiam Chang (*kiam *means 'salty'). The filling for Kiam Chang includes meat (traditionally pork), dried prawns, chestnuts, salted egg yolk, lotus seeds and Chinese mushrooms. The Cantonese rice dumpling, called Hum Yoke Choong includes streaky pork and green beans. Most of the savoury dumplings use five-spice powder for flavour. Both the Hokkiens and the Cantonese also make Kee Chang (lye water dumpling) which is smaller and has no filling; it is eaten with a thick, sweet syrup made of* gula Melaka *(coconut palm sugar) or with sugar. In what used to be the Straits Settlements of Penang, Malacca and Singapore, there is also Nonya* chang, *also referred to as Pua Kiam Tnee Chang, because the filling has salty (*kiam*) and sweet (*tnee*) ingredients that include meat, groundnuts,* tong tung kwa *(candied winter melon) and several Asian spices but not five-spice powder. There are variations in the fillings and the way Nonya* chang *is prepared in Singapore, Penang and Malacca. There are also other versions in the countries of Southeast Asia.*

This recipe for Bak Chang from my wife's aunt jee chim *is a bit different from others in that red beans are used.*

Bamboo leaves are readily available today in Asian grocery shops of Western cities. When we were in London in the Seventies and Eighties, it was difficult to find bamboo leaves. So we had to improvise by using freezer-to-boiler plastic bags to wrap our chang. *These bags, which are made of special plastic, are used to store food in the freezer. The frozen food can be conveniently boiled in water to thaw in the days before we had microwave ovens to thaw frozen food. We used a plastic sealer to seal the* chang *into the traditional dumpling shape – a pyramid. To make the plastic bag porous, we poked holes in it with a thick, sharp pin.*

A large stock pot filled with boiling water will be needed to cook the chang. *Old 10-gallon kerosene tins were once used for this purpose. There should be enough water to completely cover all the dumplings being boiled.*

Considerable time could be saved – from a few hours to 20-30 minutes – by boiling the chang *in a pressure cooker.*

Bak Chang

MAKES ABOUT 25

100 g red beans
150 g dried chestnuts,
    soaked in water
50 g dried Chinese
    mushrooms
700 g lean pork
200 g red onions
3 tbsps oil
1 kg glutinous rice
2 tbsps five-spice powder
2 tsps salt
½ tsp pepper
1 tbsp soya sauce
1 tbsp sugar
150 g dried prawns, soaked
    in water

150 g bamboo leaves
Kiam chow or rafia
1½ tbsps salt

Soak red beans and chestnuts separately overnight.

Wash the rice and soak in water for 4 hours.

Boil the chestnuts and simmer for 20 min.

Soak the mushrooms in 100 ml of water till soft. Drain, but keep the water in which the mushrooms have been soaking in for later use. Remove the stalks of the mushrooms and cut each mushroom cap into 2-4 pieces depending on the size.

Cut the pork into 2-cm cubes.

Slice the onions thinly and deep fry in the oil till golden brown.

Reserve half of the fried onions for the pork filling. Combine the remaining fried onions with the glutinous rice and the red beans.

Use the remaining oil to fry the pork cubes. Add 1 tablespoon of the five-spice powder, 1 teaspoon of salt, ¼ teaspoon of pepper, the soya sauce and sugar.

Add the reserved fried onions, the boiled chestnuts, the dried prawns, the mushrooms and the reserved mushroom water. Fry till fairly dry, remove from the wok and set aside.

Fry the red beans and rice mixture in a wok. Add 1 tablespoon of five-spice powder, 1 teaspoon of salt, and ¼ teaspoon of the pepper.

Prepare bamboo leaves and *kiam chow* by soaking them in hot water. Wipe the leaves with a damp cloth. Knot one end of all the *kiam chow* together. Hang the knotted end of the *kiam chow* on a chair or fix it to a support so that, after you have used each *kiam chow* to tie a dumpling, you will get a bunch of dumplings ready for boiling. Securing the *kiam chow* will also provide the tension that will make it easier to tie the dumplings.

To wrap the dumplings, begin by taking two bamboo leaves and overlapping them. Hold them horizontal and parallel to your body. Bring the two ends of the leaves together to form a cone. The overlapping ends of the leaves should be held away from you. Put more than 1 tablespoon of the rice and bean mixture into the cone, making sure that the tip of the cone is properly filled. Make a depression in the mixture. Fill this depression with 1–2 tablespoons of the filling, then cover the filling with more than 1 tablespoon of the rice and bean mixture, pressing down well. Fold the ends of the bamboo leaves downward to cover the cone. Wrap the sides of the leaves which have just been turned downward to seal the cone. The dumpling should be a pyramid shape.

Pull one length of *kiam chow* taut. Hold the dumpling near the mid-point of the *kiam chow* and wrap the string twice round the dumpling and secure by tying a knot. Trim the ends of the bamboo leaves to make a neat pyramid shape.

Repeat with the remaining bamboo leaves and ingredients.

Put the bunch of dumplings in a pot. Pour in enough boiling water to completely immerse all the dumplings. Boil for 4 hours. Hang up the dumplings tied as a bunch to drain and cool.

Alternatively, boil the dumplings in a pressure cooker for about 20– 30 min and leave to cool down before opening the cover. Hang up the dumplings as a bunch to cool.

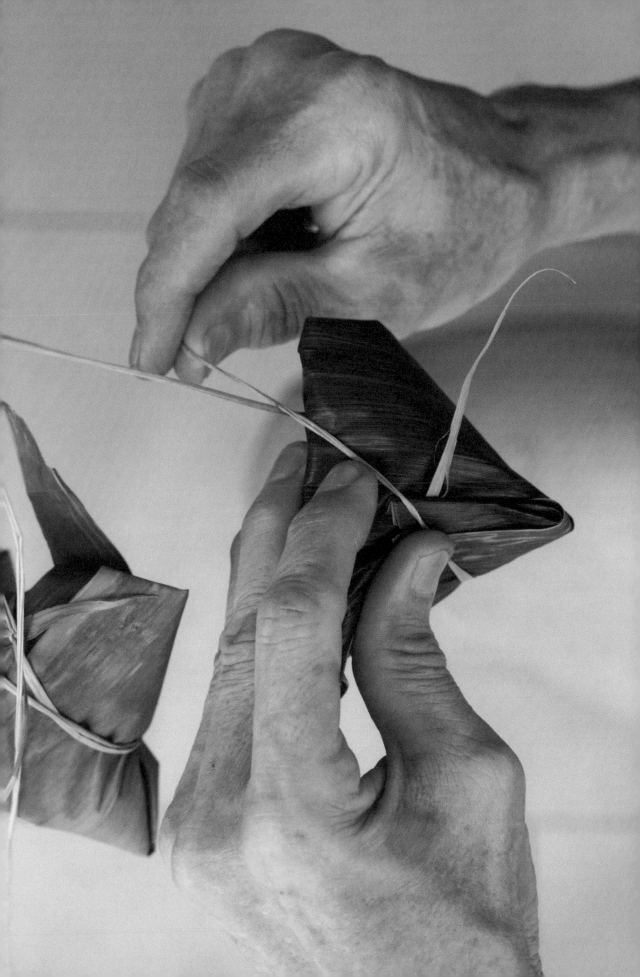

Nonya Chang NONYA-STYLE DRAGON BOAT DUMPLINGS

Nonya Chang is a variant of the savoury dumpling, Bak Chang. It is called Pua Kiam Tnee Chang in Penang and that name offers a clue to their differences. Pua kiam tnee in Hokkien means 'half salty and sweet'. The sweetness is from the chopped-up tong tung kwa or candied winter melon which is added to the dumpling's filling. The meat is either minced or diced instead of being cut into the larger pieces as for Bak Chang.

Nonya Chang has a distinctive aroma from the short length of pandan leaf used to line the bamboo-leaf wrapping. In Singapore, the leaves of the giant pandanus plant are sometimes used to wrap Nonya Chang instead of bamboo leaves.

The ingredients of ground coriander, ground pepper, garlic and shallots add spice to Nonya Chang. Many Southern Nonya recipes include dried mushrooms which are also used in Bak Chang. What distinguishes the Northern Nonya dumpling from the Southern version is the addition of cekur (lesser galangal), and pounded groundnuts.

There were discussions in the Penang Heritage Food Facebook group as to whether Penang Nonya Chang should be boiled or steamed. The consensus was that the glutinous rice is steamed till partially cooked before and after wrapping. There are not so many Penang-based recipes that ask for the glutinous rice to be boiled. In Singapore, raw glutinous rice is boiled after wrapping or it is steamed till partially cooked before wrapping and then boiled afterwards. The pua kiam tnee dumplings from Northern Malaya tend to be smaller — more chomel; those from the South, especially from Singapore, are much larger. The probable reason is that it takes a shorter time to properly steam if it is smaller.

In general, coconut milk is mixed with the steamed glutinous rice in the Northern Nonya version, while oil or lard is used to fry the raw glutinous rice with other ingredients before boiling for the Southern version.

It is quite a common practice for the Nonyas in the South to partially colour their dumplings blue using colour extracted from the bunga telang (Butterfly Pea flower). Some Nonyas in the North follow this practice only because they have relatives from Malacca.

This Penang recipe for Pua Kiam Tnee Chang is based on the one used by my father's younger brother's wife whom we call nooi chim. She told me she learned it from my tua kor (senior aunt). The filling includes lesser galangal and pounded groundnuts.

Nonya Chang

MAKES ABOUT 25

Filling
750 g belly pork
225 g groundnuts
200 g candied winter melon
  (*tong tung kwa*)

Spice Paste
4 cloves garlic
70 g shallots
15 g lesser galangal (*cekur*)
3 tbsps ground coriander
2 tsps pepper

3 tbsps oil
1 tbsp sugar
1 tbsp light soya sauce
1 tsp salt

Glutinous Rice
1 kg glutinous rice, washed
  and soaked in water for 4
  hours
200 ml coconut milk
8 pandan leaves, rinsed,
  knot 4, cut remaining into
  6-cm strips
50 bamboo leaves, soaked in
  water and wiped
25 *kiam chow*, soaked in
  water, or rafia
1 tsp sugar
A pinch of salt

Filling
Boil the belly pork in water till it is cooked. Remove the skin. Trim off the soft bits of fat but keep some of the firmer fat. Dice the pork into 5-mm cubes.

Fry the groundnuts at low heat or grill till light brown. If groundnuts with skins are used, remove the skins when cool. Pound the groundnuts coarsely. If you are using a food processor to chop the roasted groundnuts, it is unavoidable that you will end up with both finely and coarsely chopped nuts. This does not matter.

Dice the candied winter melon into 5-mm cubes.

Spice Paste
Smash the garlic, remove the skin and chop finely. Peel the shallots and chop coarsely. Scrape off the skin of the lesser galangal roots and chop coarsely.

Pound or grind the garlic, shallots and the lesser galangal roots with a mortar and pestle or food processor, then add the ground coriander, pepper and 2 tablespoons of water, and mix well. Set aside this spice paste.

Heat up a wok, add the oil and, when it is hot, add the spice paste. Sauté or, as the nonyas say, *tumis* the spice paste until it is fragrant, stirring continuously.

Add the diced belly pork and candied winter melon, sugar, light soya sauce and salt and stir till the mixture is fragrant.

Glutinous Rice
Put a steamer lined with muslin into a wok. Spread the glutinous rice evenly in the steamer. Pour boiling water over the rice so that the water drains into the wok. Spread out the rice evenly again and use the handle of a wooden spoon to make holes in the rice to allow the steam to go through, especially if the steamer is small and the layer of rice is thick.

Bring the water to a boil, cover, and steam for about

5 minutes. Stir the rice to bring the rice at the bottom of the steamer to the top. Make holes in the rice again and steam for another 5 minutes. The rice will be partially cooked at this stage.

Transfer the steamed rice into a mixing bowl and sprinkle the coconut milk evenly all over the rice. Use the wooden spoon to thoroughly mix the partially steamed rice with the coconut milk, breaking up lumps of rice with more coconut milk if necessary. Ensure that all the rice grains are coated with the coconut milk.

Transfer the rice back into the steamer, add the knotted pandan leaves, make holes in the rice and steam for 7 minutes. Stir the rice so that the rice at the bottom of the steamer is moved to the top and continue steaming for another 8 minutes.

Wrapping
See instructions on page 141.

Put the bunch of dumplings into a prepared steamer and steam for 20 minutes.

When ready, hang the dumplings by the *kiam chow* strings to drain and cool before serving.

Rempah Udang   SAVOURY PRAWN ROLLS

Rempah Udang, mispronounced as Lumpah Udang by the Penang Hokkiens, is a Nonya kuih made from glutinous rice steamed with coconut milk and wrapped in banana leaf. It has a filling of pan-fried spicy prawns – sambal udang – and fried grated coconut or kerisik, both in Malay. It is also known as Pulut Panggang to the southern Nonyas in Malacca and Singapore who often partially colour the rice blue with bunga telang. Colouring the rice blue is not a common practice in Penang.

The Malay version of Rempah Udang is similar to the Nonya version but there are distinct differences. The common ingredients used are shallots, garlic, lemongrass and kerisik. The Malay version uses tumeric and chillies which are not used in the Nonya dish. On the other hand, the Nonyas use fresh prawns, coriander, ground pepper, cekur, pandan leaves and soya sauce which are not used by the Malays. I have added some chillies to my recipe to give the filling a bit of red. There are other Malay variants of Rempah Udang like Pulut Bakar and Lemang, both of which have no filling.

Rempah Udang is a Nonya wedding speciality in Penang. For weddings, it is made in a smaller size – chomel, the Malay word meaning 'dainty' – that can be partaken in one or two bites at most.

I have seen many Rempah Udang, both real ones and in pictures in recipe books and on the Internet, but I have not seen any as elegantly wrapped, and held together using lidi, not staples, as that made my my wife's aunt whom we call jee chim. I am doing my part by recording this heritage technique here.

The Rempah Udang is grilled in a lightly oiled pan. Diluted coconut milk is sprinkled on while frying to prevent the banana leaf wrapping from becoming too dry and crinkly.

Rempah Udang

MAKES 30

Kerisik

225 g white grated coconut
   for the *kerisik*

Filling

500 g prawns
2 tbsps dried prawns
4 stalks lemongrass
150 g shallots
4 cloves garlic
25 g lesser galangal (*cekur*)
2 large red chillies
1½ tsps ground pepper
1 tbsp ground coriander
6 tbsps oil
1 tsp salt
1 tbsp light soya sauce
2 tbsps sugar
120 ml coconut milk

Rice

600 g glutinous rice
1 tsp salt
2 tsp sugar
150 ml coconut milk

6 pandan leaves, 3 for
   steaming and 3 for
   wrapping
Banana leaves, blanched in
   boiling water and cut into
   15-cm squares
Coconut midribs or tooth-
   picks, about 2.5 cm long,
   cut at a slant to sharpen
   ends

Kerisik

Heat up a wok to medium heat and spread the
grated coconut evenly in it. Fry the grated coconut,
and when it is drier, turn down the heat, otherwise
you will end up with burnt *kerisik*. It is also
important to use a frying spatula to gently move the
grated coconut around so that the *kerisik* is browned
evenly. The *kerisik* is ready when it is light brown.

Allow the *kerisik* to cool and pound with a mortar
and pestle. Set aside.

It may be convenient to prepare a big batch of *kerisik*
and keep the extra for later use.

Filling

Wash the prawns, peel and de-vein. Chop up the
prawns coarsely. Soak the dried prawns for at least 10
minutes. Drain and pound.

Use the root-ends of the lemongrass; smash these
portions and slice finely.

Peel the shallots and chop them up coarsely. Set
aside. Smash and chop up the garlic. Wash and scrape
off the brown skin of the *cekur* and chop finely.

Rinse the red chillies, remove the stalks and slice the
chillies thinly. Shake off and discard the seeds.

To make the spice paste, pound the lemongrass,
shallots, garlic, *cekur*, chillies, the ground pepper and
ground coriander in a mortar and pestle, or grind
till fine in a food processor. If using a food processor,
add 2-3 tablespoons of water to ensure that the
processor grinds effectively.

Heat up a wok, then add the oil and fry the spice
paste till fragrant.

Make a well in the centre of the spice paste and fry
the pounded dried prawns in it. Then mix the spice

paste and dried prawns thoroughly.

Add the chopped prawns together with the salt, soya sauce, and sugar and stir well. When the prawns are cooked, add the coconut milk and the *kerisik*. Fry till the filling is dry and not lumpy. Set aside the filling.

Glutinous Rice
Wash the glutinous rice till the water is clear. Cover the rice with a generous amount of water and soak the rice overnight.

Dissolve the salt and sugar in 120 ml of the coconut milk. Dilute the remainder of the coconut milk with 4 tablespoons of water. Set aside for sprinkling over the Rempah Udang when you grill them.

Get a steamer ready to steam the rice. Rinse the rice and drain away the water. Line the steaming basket with a steaming cloth.

Put the rice into the steamer and pour boiling water over it. The water will drain away. Spread out the rice evenly in the steamer. Use the handle of a wooden spoon to make holes in the rice to allow the steam to go through, especially if the steamer is small and the layer of rice is thick.

After steaming for about 10 minutes, stir the rice so that the rice at the bottom of the steamer is moved to the top. Make holes in the rice again to allow the steam to go through and steam for another 10 minutes.

Transfer the rice into a mixing bowl and sprinkle the remaining 30 ml of coconut milk evenly all over the rice. Use the wooden spoon to thoroughly mix the partially steamed rice with the coconut milk, breaking up lumps of rice with more coconut milk if necessary. Ensure that all the rice grains are coated with the coconut milk.

Transfer the rice back to the steamer. Knot 3 pandan leaves and put them in the steamer, then make holes in the rice and steam for about 7 minutes.

Stir the rice so that the rice at the bottom of the steamer is moved to the top. Continue steaming for another 8 minutes.

Assembly
Cut 3 pandan leaves into half, lengthwise, and then into 6-cm strips.

Place a strip of the pandan leaf on a banana leaf about one third away from the near edge. Spread 2 tablespoons of the glutinous rice over the length of the pandan strip and 1 tablespoon of filling on top of the rice. Roll the banana leaf over the rice to form a cylinder of rice enclosing the filling. Tighten the roll.

Alternatively, a sushi mould could be used. Fill the bottom mould with 1 tablespoon of the rice and make a depression in the middle along the length of the mould. Place a tablespoon of the filling in the depression and cover with another tablespoon of rice. Add more rice if necessary so that the Rempah Udang is more compact. Cover the mould to form a cylindrical roll. Take the Rempah Udang out of the sushi mould, place a strip of pandan leaf lengthwise on it, and wrap the banana leaf tightly around it.

Flatten the bottom of the Rempah Udang and form the roll into a triangular cross-section. Push both ends of the roll to create a sloping profile.

At one end, fold the banana leaf over one side of the triangular profile of the Rempah Udang and press to make a crease. Pin the banana leaf wrapping here with a length of coconut midrib or toothpick to secure. Repeat for the other end. Trim both ends.

To grill the Rempah Udang, heat up a lightly oiled flat pan over medium heat. Place a batch of Rempah Udang on the hot pan and brush them with the diluted coconut milk. Turn over, and brush with more diluted coconut milk. Grill all three sides of each Rempah Udang till the banana leaf wrapping is light brown in patches.

Serve the Rempah Udang hot or at room temperature.

Stoves, Ovens, Pots & Pans

Traditional Nonya kitchens in Malaya, specifically in the old Straits Settlements of Penang, Malacca and Singapore, had large, table-like platform stoves where cooking was carried out. They were made from brick and cement and usually coloured a light shade of maroon. Each platform had several built-in stoves; the number depending on the size of the house – three for a small house, and five for larger ones. There was ample space beside the stoves for placing ingredients or newly prepared food.

This was what was called *chow thau* in Penang Hokkien – the head of the kitchen, *chow* meaning 'kitchen', and *thau* being 'head'. The top of the platform was called *chow theng* – the kitchen worktop, while the rest of the kitchen was called *chow kah*, the bottom of the kitchen.

One side of the space below the stoves was for storing cooking utensils and the other side or the bottom was for keeping firewood together with the utensils for cutting the wood and starting the fire – a chopper, a metal pipe for blowing streams of air to help get the fire going, and iron tongs for moving the burning wood.

My grandmothers' houses at Macalister Road and at Tanjong Tokong in Penang had big kitchen platforms. Even our family house in Jones Road had one, including a chimney in the kitchen, when it was newly built in the early 1950s. Later on, when it was not so convenient to cook with firewood, and my mother swtiched to kerosene stoves, the platform was demolished.

So, I was pleasantly surprised to see one of these kitchen platforms still being used when I visited my cousin's aunt in Takupa near Phuket in Thailand. The differences are that the *chow teng* is tiled, and gas stoves have replaced the *hung lor* for cooking.

CHARCOAL STOVE AND TONGS USED TO MOVE COALS. THE CHOPPER IS USED TO BREAK UP LARGE PIECES OF CHARCOAL.

The *hung lor* is a charcoal stove. The old-fashioned ones look like buckets lined with cement, with a rectangular opening at the lower half to allow air to flow through to the charcoal to keep it burning. It is this air vent that gives this stove its name as *hung lor* in Hokkien means 'wind stove' in Chinese. A metal or ceramic grill separates the top and the bottom part of the stove. The burning charcoal sits on the grill that allows the ashes to fall through to collect at the bottom. The heat from the charcoal can be controlled by increasing or decreasing the amount of charcoal in the stove or using a fan to boost the fire. This is all very basic.

Nowadays, the *hung lor* is mainly used for preparing dishes that need to be cooked for a long time over a slow fire, like Kaya and Kiam Chai Ark or for double boiling nutritious tonics like bird's nest soup and herbal brews. Stoves are also used to heat Kuih Bahulu moulds and to grill dried cuttlefish.

We later replaced these basic stoves with the Japanese charcoal stoves which are more sophisticated. They have sliding windows to regulate the air flow to the charcoal, thus effectively controlling the heat generated by the stove. There is another innovation which I did not know of until I accidentally broke one. When I examined the pieces, I found that the stove has an outer and inner layer with an insulating gap in between. I then realised that the insulation is for conserving energy, and for keeping the outside of the stoves at a lower temperature.

OVEN EVOLUTION

In the charcoal age, the Nonyas used large *bok keng* (*blangah* or clay pots) for baking. A large clay pot was placed over a charcoal stove. The clay pot was partially filled with sand and then lined with newspaper on the inside. The item to be baked was then put into the pot which would be covered with a metal sheet on which burning charcoal was placed. The principle is the same – use charcoal to give heat from the top and the bottom – much like how two clay pots are used to make Apong or brass moulds for Kuih Bahulu. I have also heard of baking using the same principle in large, 10-gallon kerosene tins that were common in those days.

Such clay pot and make-shift ovens were not suitable for large-scale baking, especially during the run-up to Chinese New Year. That is why my paternal grandmother sent her sugee cakes to the Indian bakery at one end of Penang Road for baking.

When the kerosene stove was introduced, baking at home became more convenient. Mother had twin kerosene stoves in the early Fifties. She also had an oven attachment which was placed over stoves so that, for the first time, she could bake cakes at home with good control over the temperature.

Kerosene stoves are still used in many developing countries. The company that sells the well-known Buttterfly brand stove is based in Singapore.

The electric cooker with hot plates, grill and oven replaced the kerosene stove oven in the 1950s. The Baby Belling cooker was popular at that time. It consisted of an electric hot plate with a small oven below.

My father worked for the Electricity Supply Department of the then Georgetown Municipal Council. We were probably one of the first few households in Penang to rent a cooker from the Electricity Supply Department that was trying to encourage the use of electricity then. I remember that it was a GEC cooker. I saw the same model advertised in the 1953 *Straits Times Annual*. My sister still uses a later GEC model for baking in our old house today.

Now, we have ovens with heating from the top, bottom and the sides, as well as grills and fans, for total control of temperature. There are also other modern ovens and stoves. The turbo-broiler, a very convenient and compact oven for baking, was invented in the 1970s. It has a large, metal or glass bowl with a removable cover with an electrical heating element and a fan to circulate and control the heat in the bowl. A more recent innovation for turbo-boilers is the introduction of halogen lamps for browning.

The microwave oven, which became a common household item from the 1980s, optionally incorporates convection ovens that make baking more convenient. You can even get one with a steamer today.

Heating without hotplates was available for the home kitchen from 2000. These induction cookers are electronically controlled and also energy efficient. They provide instant power control from low to very high at the touch of a button. The low power control is very useful for making Ban Chien Koay. It is not commonly known that to use an induction cooker, the bottom of the cooking vessel used must be magnetic. Some cooking utensils made from stainless steel are not magnetic.

KLIM MILK POWDER CONTAINERS AS BAKING TINS

From my grandmother's days, KLIM was a very well-known brand of milk powder in our part of the world. It is made by a Danish company which has been taken over by Nestle. KLIM is 'milk' spelt backwards.

My grandmother used the 1-lb KLIM containers as cake tins when she baked Sugee Cake for Chinese New Year. It was just the right size – about 11 cm in diameter. My uncle Runny mentioned to me that his favourite cake is made from the left-over sugee batter baked in an old cigarette tin!

POTS AND PANS
Wok

The Chinese wok is a very versatile, round-bottomed cooking vessel, with loop handles opposite to each other, used for a wide range of cooking techniques like stir frying, deep frying, steaming, stewing and braising. Known as *kuali* in Malaysia and Singapore, it is commonly used not only by the Chinese but also the Malays and Indians. It is also widely used in the rest of Southeast Asia. In the Philippines, it is known by a similar sounding name – *kawali*. In India, the traditional wok with a larger diameter is known as *cheena chatti* ('Chinese pot' in Tamil). They also have a similar smaller but deeper vessel called *karahi*. The wok in Japan is called *chukanabe* or 'Chinese pot'. A long-handled ladle, called *chien si* in Penang Hokkien, is used to cook with a wok.

The traditional wok is made of cast iron. Some are made from carbon steel. More recently, woks have been made from hard anodised aluminium which is very much harder than the untreated aluminium. In Thailand, the equivalent of the wok is more commonly fashioned from sheets of brass, while the looped handles are riveted – all handmade. The handles of the Indian wok are made from brass rods. The Nonyas use woks made of brass – *tung thnia* in Penang Hokkien. Some of these pans, which are quite large (about 50 cm), do not have any handles and the brass used is thinner than the other much heavier brass pans with handles. Sesargon – slow-fried grated coconut mixed with ground rice – is prepared in a *tung thnia*.

The important property of the material used to make woks is heat conductivity. That is why copper, brass, aluminium and iron are employed. The wok must also be heavy to retain the heat hence brass and cast iron are commonly used.

Pots

The traditional cylindrical pots without handles used by Nonyas for cooking are made of aluminium. These pots probably originated from India. My mother also used enamel pots of different sizes. We still use the very large ones for preparing Kiam Chye Thng. The enamel pots, like other enamelware, were made in Japan and Eastern Europe. We only switched to the western deep pan with a handle in the 1980s.

In the past, rice was cooked in a simple cooking pot. Nowadays, the rice cooker is so ubiquitous that the younger generation wouldn't know how to cook rice without it!

My mother also used clay pots, or *bok keng* in Penang Hokkien and *blangah* in Malay,

INDIAN CLAYPOTS SITTING ON POT HOLDERS WOVEN FROM THE MIDRIBS OF COCONUT LEAFLETS.

for cooking. The clay pot most probably originated from India, although they are also made locally in Malaya. For cooking Laksa, Mother used a large *bok keng* but for everyday curries, she used a smaller one. I find it better to use a large *bok keng* to cook curry as it is easier to *tumis* (sauté) the *rempah*. My mother also cooked Tau Eu Bak in a *bok keng*.

In the old days, as described above, a very large *blangah* was used as an oven for baking. The *blangah* is still used today, but the quality could be improved. My cousin advised me to bring a bottle of water when choosing *blangah*, to check that the pot is not leaking before paying for it.

Double Boiler

A double boiler consists of a pot within a pot, hence its name. A pot with a smaller diameter sits inside and on top of another one. There is space at the bottom and a small gap between the sides of the two pots. The main contact between the two vessels is therefore the boiling water in the space between them. In our Science lessons in school, this is a water bath. Most of the double boilers that I have seen in my young days are made of enamel but later ones are made of aluminium and, more recently, of stainless steel.

A double boiler is used for cooking food at a constant temperature of 100°C, the boiling point of water, a temperature that will not destroy nutrients. Traditionally, it is used for a number of classic dishes: bird's nest soup or chicken soup, herbal tonics and Kaya. For Kaya, the egg and coconut milk mixture is initially cooked at a low temperature and then double boiled for a few hours.

Steamboat

The traditional steamboat or *ean lor* in Penang Hokkien is handmade from sheets of copper or brass. They are made with simple tools and a lot of skill. In 2014, I was surprised to see a metalsmith making one in his workshop in Chulia Street, Penang. With the gentrification of the street, and the casting of steamboats from aluminum, I wonder how long the trade will survive.

The steamboat has three detachable parts. The bottom part is the charcoal stove. The middle part, which has a circular trough to cook food and a ventilation funnel at the centre, sits on the stove so that the trough is in close contact with the heat from the

A BRASS STEAMBOAT. THE SMALL NET IS ALSO CONVENIENT FOR SCOOPING OUT ONDEH ONDEH (PAGE 92) AFTER THEY HAVE BEEN BOILED.

burning charcoal. The third part is a cover with two handles for putting it on and lifting it off the cooking trough. Like the *hung lor*, the stove has an adjustable vent on the side to control the heat by adjusting the amount of air going into the stove.

In my student days, we used a rice cooker as our steamboat; we had to be patient because the power ratings for rice cookers are not that high. These days, placing a pot over an induction cooker makes a good steamboat substitute as induction cookers have high power ratings and the ability to control the heating quickly.

Most steamboats used in restaurants today use gas for heating. Electric steamboats are quite common too, including ones which incorporate grills for barbecue.

In the past, an important accessory to the steamboat was a palm leaf fan used to rouse the charcoal fire. At the Teochew restaurant in Kimberley Street, Penang, where traditional charcoal steamboats are used, you are provided with a battery-operated fan instead – the traditional and the modern!

STEAMER

Steaming is an important way of cooking Nonya *kuih*. Traditional steamers are made of bamboo, but Nonyas tend to use aluminium steamers. The water is boiled in a wok and two layers of the steamers with holes in their bottoms are stacked on top, together with the cover. The steam from the boiling water rises through the holes and gets trapped by the cover to cook the food.

WIRE SIEVE

Traditional wire sieves, or *he-ir* in Penang Hokkien, have baskets made of brass wire and handles made of bamboo. More recently, stainless steel wire has been used.

The shallow sieve is used in Wantan Mee stalls in the process of blanching the noodles, transferring them from boiling water to a basin of cold water and then back to the hot water again. It is also used as a sieve to drain oil from deep-fried food, like *keropok*, Choon Piah (Hainanese spring roll) and Roti Babi.

A deeper sieve, also made of bamboo and brass wire, is used by hawkers for blanching noodles for Hokkien Mee, Koay Teow Thng, Mee Rebus and Mee Goreng.

A small version of this seive is used at steamboat dinners to fish out the food without the soup. I use this to pick up Ondeh-Ondeh from boiling water and to drain off the water before rolling the balls of dough in grated coconut.

TRAYS AND PLATES

Trays, or *dulang* in Malay, used by the Nonyas are traditionally made of brass or enamel and come in different sizes. The more common enamel trays are still used today for drying ingredients like *keropok*, *ikan bilis*, dried prawns, and vegetables used for Acar Awak.

Enamel trays were also used for sorting polished rice from glutinous rice.

Enamel plates are handy to have in a kitchen for preparing ingredients and keeping aside small amounts of foodstuff. They are also convenient as small steaming trays.

IRON TONGS, BLOW-PIPE, AND FIREWOOD CHOPPER

Iron tongs are indispensable for managing fires that burn firewood or charcoal. When baking Kuih Bahulu for example, it is needed to put burning charcoal onto the cover of the mould as well as to lift the hot cover off. Similar transfers are also needed for the old-fashioned ovens using *blangah* (clay pots) and metal sheet covers.

Metal pipes were used to blow air to help start a fire. The results were somewhat disastrous if the pipe was not removed from the mouth when taking in a deep breath!

A heavy chopper was used to cut firewood. Those living in town used bakau wood while those living in the more *ulu* ('remote' in Malay) areas used rubber or any other available wood. My wife told me about someone in the Kee family estate who virtually spent all his time chopping firewood for the families in the community.

Sugee Cake SEMOLINA CAKE

Sugee *or* sooji *is a North Indian name for semolina which is made from a hard, yellow wheat called* durum. *A different product, called* farina, *is made from a softer white wheat.*

When you bite into a piece of Sugee Cake you can feel the texture of the semolina, the crunch of the almonds, as well as the finely chopped dried fruits.

This recipe for Sugee Cake is from my mother. It originated from my Tanjong Tokong grandmother on my father's side of the family. Coarser semolina, the key ingredient, distinguishes the cake from cakes baked with only flour. Some brands of sugee are coarser than others; the coarser ones are preferred. The original recipe includes many other ingredients: Almond, keat piah *(preserved kamquat),* tong tung kwa *(candied winter melon), nutmeg flesh, and several ground spices – nutmeg, ginger, cinnamon, fennel and cumin. Brandy and several essences like almond, vanilla and rose were also used, the last suggesting influences from the Ceylon Muslims or even the Moors of Spain and Portugal in the Middle Ages.*

My recollection of Sugee Cake from my grandmother's day is that it had strong flavours of spice and rose essence. Over the years, the amount of spices added has been reduced. My mother's version has fewer spices and my wife's doesn't use rose essence, is less oily, and not so sweet. We now have variations of the recipe in the different branches of my paternal family.

Sugee Cake is a popular cake among the Eurasians in what was the Straits Settlements of Penang, Malacca and Singapore. The cake is baked for festive occasions like Christmas, Chinese New Year and birthdays. The Eurasian recipes are simpler, without the spices, dried fruits and peels, but calls for a covering of icing. It is not commonly known that the Nonyas have their own version, which is more spicy and includes several candied fruits and peels.

In researching the origins of Sugee Cake, I found a very similar Greek cake called Revani. It uses the flavours of cinnamon stick, cloves and orange peel as well as vanilla extract and brandy. Almonds are also used as an ingredient – chopped and slivered, the latter for the top of the cake with marachino cherry slices.

My cousin referred me to a recipe for Love Cake. It is a popular Sri Lankan semolina cake adopted from the Portuguese who dominated the spice trade in what was then called Ceylon in the 16th century, or from the Dutch who arrived later. This could explain why spices were added to the Sugee Cake made by my grandmother. Another similarity is that the Sri Lankans add crystallized pumpkin while my grandmother used crystalline winter melon. Candied pumpkin, called puhul dosi *in Sri Lanka, was most probably adapted from the Portuguese squash preserve* doce de chila, *reinforcing the Portuguese connection.*

The old Straits Settlements recipes for Sugee Cake use almonds while the Sri Lankan recipes use cashew nuts which was readily available locally. The ground spices used in the Sri Lankan recipes include cardamom, cinnamon, clove and nutmeg. Our recipe for Sugee Cake has nutmeg, ginger, cinnamon, fennel and cummin. The spice mix in Mrs Leong Yee Soo's Sugee

Cake recipe consists of cinnamon, cloves, star anise and cardamon.

While sugee is used with a small portion of flour in Love Cake – 100 g self-raising flour in one case – some recipes do not use flour at all.

However, there is a big difference between Sri Lankan Love Cake and my grandmother's Sugee Cake. While the Sri Lankans toast their semolina, our family recipe calls for the semolina to be soaked in butter for several hours. The latter is done so that the semolina is not too hard.

Adam Balic, an authority on the history of cooking, referred me to two old recipes similar to Sugee Cake. The first, for Portuguese Almond Cake, published in 1900 in The People's Indian Cookery Book by Olivia C Fitzgerald, has sugee, butter, finely ground almonds, eggs, sugar and rose water. It also has the instruction that "the egg whites are to be beaten to a froth". This, of course, as all bakers know, is to help the cake rise.

The second, a recipe for a favourite cake for Christmas, weddings, birthdays, and christenings in India, is given in Indian Cookery Book, published c1900. The ingredients, besides that given for the Portuguese Almond Cake are: Flour, preserved ginger, citron, orange-peel, lemon-peel and pumpkin – all cut into small pieces and well dried; cinnamon – finely pounded and sifted; nutmegs – finely grated; English caraway-seeds – cleaned and picked; Mace – finely pounded and sifted; and dried orange-peel – also finely pounded and sifted. The almonds are blanched and finely sliced.

According to Adam, Portuguese Cakes have a very long tradition in English cookery – early 18th century, most likely earlier – and are in fact English. He suggested that the recipe is so old that the cake is no longer made in Portugal, and that the recipe was developed in the colonies. Although these cakes do not use semolina, they are an important group of recipes – early examples of cakes that use eggs.

Early 18th century Portuguese Cakes recipes used currant but later ones include almond and brandy. There is a similar Goan cake called Batega which uses sugee, and coconut instead of almond.

So there is sufficient evidence to suggest that Sugee Cake originated from the Indian sub-continent with a lot of Portuguese and English influences.

I can still remember how Sugee Cake was made during my grandmother's time in our Tanjong Tokong house. The baking was done just before Chinese New Year. The ladies of the household would wake up early to prepare the cake mixture. Much effort had been made several days earlier to chop up and dry the ingredients.

When the cake mix was ready, it was poured into re-cycled one-pound KLIM milk tins lined with grease-proof paper.

In those days, there were no facilities for large-scale baking at home, so the tins of the cake mix were sent down by trishaw to an Indian bakery near the Catholic Church in Penang Road. The temperature of the oven in the bakery was a bit variable. If we were lucky, the cakes would come out fine, but, occasionally, there would be some dark or burnt cakes and even darker faces!

Sugee Cake

This recipe requires three
450 g loaf tins

100 g almonds
250 g semolina (*sugee*)
350 g butter
6 egg yolks
3 egg whites
250 g sugar
100 g self-raising flour,
sifted
25 g preserved kamquat
(*keat piah*), coarsely
chopped
25 g preserved nutmeg flesh,
coarsely chopped
25 g candied winter melon
(*tong tung kwa*), coarsely
chopped
¼ tsp ground ginger
¼ tsp grated nutmeg
½ tsp almond essence
½ tsp vanilla essence
1½ tbsps brandy

Blanch the almonds in boiling water and remove the skins. Slice some of the almonds thinly to decorate the top of the cake and set aside to dry. Chop up the rest of the almonds.

Blend the semolina with softened butter for 5-7 minutes until the mixture is fluffy. Set aside.

Separate 6 egg yolks from the whites.

Beat the egg whites and add the sugar. Continue beating till there is no liquid at the bottom of the bowl and the whites are firm. The beaten egg white should not flow out when the bowl is inverted.

Beat 6 yolks, one at a time, and mix with the semolina and butter mixture until fluffy. Set aside. Combine the self-raising flour, the chopped almond, the preserved kamquat, nutmeg flesh, candied winter melon, ground ginger and grated nutmeg.

Add the essences and the brandy into the mixture of yolks and butter. Fold in the flour, fruit and spice mixture and add the beaten egg whites. Mix well, and transfer the cake mix to the three loaf tins which have been lined with grease-proof paper.

Spread the sliced almonds on top of the cake mixture.

Preheated an oven to 175°C. Bake the cakes for 10 minutes, then reduce the temperature to 150°C and continue baking for about 40 minutes. The cakes are ready when the cakes shrink away from the sides slightly. Insert a skewer into the cakes. They are ready when the skewer comes out clean. Cover the tops of the cakes with aluminium foil if they become brown before they have cooked through.

When done, allow to cool for about 10 minutes before removing the cakes from the tins to rest on to a wire rack.

Almond Drops

MAKES 50

Almond Drops is one of the cookies that my late mother used to bake. It is suitable for serving during Chinese New Year. Technically, the spherical dough is dropped on to a baking tray and, when baked, will settle into a more circular shape. However, we like it thinner so we flatten the dough before baking.

My cousin, S Yoong and I decided to make it a few years ago. We had not done it by ourselves before. We had a problem. The recipe we were working with used cup measure for all the ingredients except butter which was specified in weight. This is a very typical problem with old recipes; we were not sure what size cups we were supposed to use. We found out by trial and error that we didn't use enough flour. The almond drop mixture was a bit runny, difficult to handle but it tasted fine – more buttery!

From my earliest recollection, my mother baked using a kerosene stove that had an oven sitting on it. In the early 1950s, that was already an advancement over what was used before, with better control over the oven temperature. Before the kerosene stove ovens, a large claypot filled with sand, which served as an oven, was heated from below and above using charcoal. Experience gained from a lot of trial and error was needed to control these early claypot ovens. I have some experience using the Kuih Bahulu mould which also has charcoal heating from below and above (see page 206).

Towards the mid-1950s, my mother started using an electric oven. We were what is known today as early adaptors because my father worked for the Electric Supply Department of the Georgetown Municipal Council that promoted the use of electricity!

60 g sugar **½ tsp salt** **240 g butter**	Combine the sugar, salt and the butter until creamy and pale in colour.
300 g flour **120 g ground almonds**	Mix the flour and the ground almonds to form a soft dough. Transfer the dough onto a well-floured worktop. Form the dough into a cylinder about 2 cm in diameter and cut it into 2-cm pieces. Roll each portion into a ball, drop on a lined baking tray and flatten to about 1 cm.
	Leave a 2-3 cm space between the dough on the baking tray as they will expand when baked.
	Bake at 175°C for about 15 minute till the bottom edges are golden brown but not the top.
	Allow to cool on the baking tray and then serve, or store in a sealed container.

Red Agar Agar Eggs

MAKES 10

In many cultures both Eastern and Western, eggs signify a new beginning or a new life.

The infant mortality rate in the past in China was high, hence if a baby survived the first month of life, the event is significant. It is still celebrated by giving hardboiled eggs coloured red to relatives and friends. In Chinese culture, red signifies prosperity and good fortune.

In Malay culture, the egg is a symbol of fertility, hence eggs have a prominent place in a wedding, symbolizing a fertile union between the couple. The practice of giving hardboiled eggs has evolved from just giving eggs, to presenting the eggs in baskets known as bunga telur, *to the more modern practice of giving other gifts instead of eggs.*

In Western culture, Easter and eggs are almost synonymous. Easter wouldn't be the same today without Easter eggs. In the Orthodox Church, red Easter eggs symbolize Christ's resurrection. Onion skins are boiled to produce the red dye to colour the eggs red.

My late mother made Red Agar Agar Eggs using empty egg shells and agar agar flavoured with rose essence. I thought that these eggs will go well in a baby's first month celebration, so I made some for my first grandchild, Alice Ong, when we celebrated her turning one-month old.

You will need empty shells and the egg box used to pack the eggs. Carefully make a small hole about 1 cm in diameter whenever you need to cook eggs. Shake the egg gently to extract the egg yolk and white. It may be easier to break the yolk. Clean and dry the egg shells and keep aside.

10 empty egg shells
600 ml water
25 g agar agar, soaked
50 g sugar
Red colouring
1 tsp rose essence

Arrange the 10 empty egg shells with holes facing upwards in the egg box. Get a small funnel for filling the empty egg shells with the agar agar.

Boil the water and then dissolve the agar agar in it. Stir in the sugar. When the sugar has dissolved, add the red colouring and stir well. Turn off the heat and, when it is not so hot, add the rose essence.

Use a funnel to fill each egg shell to the brim. Let the eggs cool down before placing them in the refrigerator to set.

Before serving, crack the egg shells and discard the shells.

Kow Chan Kuih NINE-LAYER CAKE

Kow Chan Kuih or Kuih Lapis may have a Malay origin since the main ingredients – rice and coconut – are plentiful in the kampongs of the Malayan Peninsula. However, there is a more plausible suggestion that it may have originated from a Hokkien koay *(cake), also called Kow Chan Koay, which is made of glutinous rice and sugar and is coloured the same pink and white as the Penang Kow Chan Kuih.*

Kow Chan Kuih, which means 'nine layer cake' is also known as Kuih Lapis in Penang. The nine layers have symbolic associations to bu bu gao sheng [步步高升] *and* bu bu zhang jin [步步长进] *which mean 'promotion' and 'growing up or developing maturity' respectively. In Chinese, the pronounciation of the number nine sounds similar to the character for 'long' or 'old', suggesting longevity. As such, the diamond-shaped Kow Chan Kuih was often served at the 60th birthday of the family patriarch or matriach. It was also one of the kuihs served in traditional Nonya weddings in Penang, taking its place among Kuih Bengka, Huat Kuih, Pulut Taitai and Ondeh Ondeh, just to name a few.*

Kow Chan Kuih should not be confused with the other Kuih Lapis from Indonesia with Dutch origins which is cake-like and baked, not steamed. There is, however, a similar cake of nine layers made by Chinese of the Hakka dialect to celebrate the Double Ninth Festival on the ninth day of the ninth month when they practice the custom of climbing hills to admire the chrysanthemums in bloom. This cake is brown and cut in diamond shapes, which supports the view of my Facebook friend Katy Biggs who suggested that the original colour of Kow Chan Kuih was brown, not pink.

The Nonyas could have adapted the Chinese Kow Chan Koay by using local products, replacing the glutinous rice with ordinary rice flour, green bean flour and tapioca flour to improve the texture. Many recipes, especially the Nonya ones, use mainly tapioca flour and/or sago flour, which give the kuih *a chewy texture. Only rice flour and green bean flour are used in this recipe which was demonstrated to me by my wife's aunt whom we call* jee chim *who used to make Nonya kuihs for weddings. The recipe was fine-tuned by me.*

Kow Chan Kuih is made by steaming the nine layers of the kuih *batter layer by layer. What distinguishes the Penang version from the Malacca, Singapore and Indonesian varieties is the colour. The Penang* kuih *has alternate pink and white layers topped with a reddish orange layer. Many of the versions from the other territories are colourful, including green, blue and even purple! In Susie Hing's* A Malayan Kitchen, *white, green, pink and dark pinks were the colours used in her Kwei Lapis recipe. She originated from Indonesia.*

Penang Kow Chan Kuih is traditionally cut into diamond shapes. When I was young, my siblings and I peeled the kuih *and ate it layer by layer; a well-made Kow Chan Kuih must allow you to do that. It should also be* al dente *and not chewy. It is the green bean flour that gives it that texture.*

I came across references to Kuih Lapis Cerai while researching Kow Chan Kuih or Kuih Lapis. I then found out that cerai means 'divorce' in Malay and wondered what divorce has to do with Kow Chan Kuih. Perhaps it refers to the ease of separating the layers of this kuih. With nine layers you can do it eight times – I am not sure whether this is legal!

Circular trays were used to make Kow Chan Kuih because steaming trays were all circular. Since the kuih is cut into diamond shapes, there is some wastage. However, from the kitchen helpers' point of view, it is a bonus! My cousin showed me a diamond shaped tray that was specially made by my Uncle Teng Boon for his wife, my tua kor or eldest paternal aunt, to eliminate any wastage.

For this recipe, use a 24 cm square tray or a round tray with a diameter of about 24.5 cm and 4-5 cm deep.

I have not been so lucky making Kow Chan Kuih. Something would go wrong during the numerous occasions when I tested and fine-tuned this recipe. Once, the steamer ran dry. On another occasion, the layers were of uneven thickness. Perhaps I should say that, on occasion, I had not been very careful when making Kow Chan Kuih. You can learn from my mistakes.

Kow Chan Kuih

400 g rice flour
75 g green bean flour
  (*lek tau hoon*)
50 g tapioca flour
500 g grated coconut OR
  250 ml thick coconut
  milk
350 g sugar
5 pandan leaves
Red food colouring
Yellow food colouring

Sieve the rice flour, the green bean flour and the tapioca flour together into a mixing bowl. Mix thoroughly with 600 ml of water. Leave this liquid flour mixture aside.

If you are using grated coconut, squeeze 250 ml of coconut milk from the grated coconut. Set aside. Add 300 ml of water to the squeezed coconut and squeeze again for the second squeeze milk and set this aside as well. Repeat with another 300 ml of water for the third squeeze milk. Combine the second and third squeeze coconut milk and leave aside.

Alternatively, if you are using commercial thick coconut milk, use 600 ml of water instead of the second and third coconut squeeze.

Combine the second and third squeeze coconut milk with the sugar and the pandan leaves in a pot and bring to a boil. When the sugar has dissolved, remove the pandan.

Stir in the liquid flour mixture and then the thick coconut milk. Mix thoroughly and sieve to remove any lumps.

Weigh this batter and divide it into 9 equal portions in separate bowls. Colour 4 portions pink by mixing in 6 drops of red colouring. Colour the one portion for the top layer with 8 drops of red colouring and 1 drop of yellow colouring. Leave 4 portions uncoloured.

Steaming
Put a steamer into a wok. Pour enough water into the wok to bring the water level to 5 cm below the steamer. Cover the steamer and bring the water to a simmer.

Oil a steaming tray and place it in the steamer to heat up.

When the water is steaming, take the cover off the steamer and wipe away the condensation formed in it to prevent liquid from dripping onto the layers of the *kuih*.

Pour in one portion of the pink batter. Adjust the steamer so that the tray is level. This is to ensure that the thickness for each layer of the *kuih* will be uniform.

Prick the bubbles that may have formed.

Steam for 5-7 minutes till the pink layer becomes a deeper shade of pink and is firm to the touch.

Pour in a portion of the uncoloured batter, cover the steamer and allow to steam for another 5-7 minutes. The uncoloured layer will become a shade of white when it is ready.

Repeat with alternating pink and uncoloured batters.

Check that there is sufficient water in the steamer regularly and top up to make sure that the steamer does not run dry. Wipe away the condensation from the inside of the cover before replacing it.

The last reddish-orange layer of batter should be steamed for 5-7 minutes. The cover is taken off for about a minute then the Kow Chan Kuih is steamed again for a further 5 minutes with the cover on.

Wipe off the condensation from under the cover. Put the cover back on the steamer and leave the *kuih* to cool down and become firm up before slicing.

Slice into strips, length-wise, with a corrugated knife, and then at a slant to obtain diamond shaped Kow Chan Kuih.

Do let your kitchen helpers enjoy the trimmings!

Kaya COCONUT AND EGG JAM

Kaya is also known as Serikaya in Malaysia, Singapore and Indonesia. It is called Sangkhaya in Thailand and Matamís Sa Bao in the Philippines. For vegetarians, there are kayas which use pumpkin or yam instead of egg. The Filipino Matamís Sa Bao doesn't use egg.

Coconut and egg jam is a good description for our Kaya which is traditionally made by slow cooking a mixture of egg, sugar and coconut milk, and steaming for several hours. The jam is flavoured by pandan leaves. The sugar and the steaming preserves the Kaya so that it can keep longer in the days before refrigerators.

Like other jams, it is spread over fresh or buttered toast for breakfast. Kaya on toast is traditionally served with half-boiled eggs in kopitiams *(coffee shops) which were run by the Hainaneses in Malaysia and Singapore.*

Kaya and Pulut Taitai (see page 231) goes together like a horse and carriage; Kaya is spread over thin slices of the steamed blue and white marbled glutinous rice. Kuih Salat is another Malay and Nonya kuih *which is topped with a Kaya mix. There is also a Sri Lankan Muslim dessert, Vattalappam, which is basically Serikaya but flavoured with cardoman instead of pandan leaves. It is garnished with cashew nuts.*

Kaya is a Malay word meaning 'rich'. It could refer to the richness of Serikaya, culinary-wise. This suggests that Kaya has Malay origins and was adopted by the Nonyas. However, there are suggestions that Kaya may have evolved from the Portuguese Ovos Moles, which is made from a mix of sugar and egg, cooked over a low heat. Ovos Moles is served as a dessert by itself or spread over sponge cake.

I grew up with the traditional golden or reddish-brown Kaya which is the result of the caramelisation of sugar. My recipe here produces this style of Kaya. There is also a green Kaya which is coloured by pandan-leaf extract. There is a theory on the Internet that the green Kaya is Nonya and the golden brown version is Hainanese. You cannot believe everything you read on the World Wide Web! Most of the recipes of Serikaya in classical Nonya cookbooks use pandan only for flavouring and not for colouring. The Hainaneses most probably learnt to make Kaya from the Nonyas because many of them worked for the rich Nonya families as full-time cooks.

The preparation of Kaya needs extra care because both the egg and the coconut milk curdle easily if the temperature is too high. Make a mistake and you may get lumpy Kaya or, worse still, scrambled eggs!

Traditionally, a double boiler is used to cook Kaya. You will need a lot of patience to continuously stir the mixture. My Facebook friend Cheryll Ng said that her mother-in-law lit a joss stick and stopped stirring only when it had burnt out. What you must look for is the thickening of the mixture and the colour changing from pale cream to a translucent, darker colour. The Kaya can then be further cooked in the double-boiler or it could be transferred to a metal container and steamed for a few more hours.

For steaming, place the container with the cooked egg and coconut milk mixture on a rack in a wok or a large pot. Wrap a cloth round the underside of the cover to prevent any condensed water from falling on the Kaya and ruining the surface.

The steaming time will determine the colour and the texture of the Kaya; it becomes darker, thicker and less creamy the longer it is steamed. We could shorten the process by caramelising some of the sugar or using gula Melaka to give your Kaya a golden brown finish. If you like your Kaya more solid, steam it for longer.

For those fortunate enough to own one, a Thermomix will take away the tedium of stirring and the steaming; the machine can control temperature, timing and stirring.

One bowl of eggs, one bowl of sugar, and one bowl of coconut milk is a good rule of thumb for the proportion of ingredients for making Kaya.

Kaya

10 eggs
600 g fine sugar, set aside
    4 tbsp for caramelising
500 ml coconut milk

Use an absorbent cloth to line the underside of the cover of the double boiler or the cover of the container used for steaming.

Beat the eggs well using an egg beater or a cake mixer. Use a sieve to remove any white strands which tend to stick to the beater. Add the sugar to the egg and stir till the sugar has almost all melted.

Now include the coconut milk and stir till the sugar has melted completely. Use your thumb and forefinger to feel the mixture; the sugar is not all dissolved if you feel sugar crystals.

Pour the mixture into a double boiler. Adjust the heat so that only some steam escapes from between the bottom and top pots of the boiler. Stir especially the bottom and sides of the pot continuously until the creamy egg mixture turns translucent and darker.

To caramelise the sugar, put the 4 tablespoons of sugar in a pot and cook over medium heat. Stir with a wooden spoon till the sugar melts. Then turn down the heat and continue to stir till the sugar is light brown. If the sugar boils, quickly remove from fire.

Pour the hot, creamy egg mixture into the pot of caramelised sugar and stir continuously to ensure that the sugar blends in.

Now pour the Kaya mixture back into the top part of the double boiler and continue to cook for 30 minutes Then stir thoroughly and steam for another 30 minutes. At this stage, your Kaya is ready if you prefer it more liquid. If you prefer it firmer, thoroughly stir the Kaya and steam for a further 30 minutes or more to get the texture you like. Ensure that the water in the bottom pot is refilled.

Alternatively, pour the Kaya mixture into a metal container and steam, following the procedure for the double boiler. Ensure there is water for steaming.

Transfer into bottles for storage.

Bubur Cha Cha   COCONUT MILK DESSERT

Bubur Cha Cha is a dessert that evolved from Pengat, a traditional Malay sweet dish cooked with coconut milk, gula Melaka *and various fruits and root vegetables. Thus, there is Pengat Pisang using banana, Pengat Labu with pumpkin, and Pengat Keladi that has yam. The Nonyas adopted this dessert and, combining bananas, yam and sweet potatoes, called their version simply Pengat.*

Pengat is a Nonya festive dessert like Kuih Ee, taken by the Nonyas during Chap Goh Meh, the fifteen day of Chinese New Year. Thus, much care was taken in cutting the yam and sweet potatoes into precise shapes and sizes. There are some Nonyas who don't consider it proper to serve Pengat at other times of the year. That is the very probable reason why Pengat was modified to become Bubur Cha Cha, a dessert that can be eaten any day of the year, and even sold by hawkers.

An article about Bubur Cha Cha and Pengat by Lin Suan Har in the Pulau Pinang *magazine says that yam and sweet potatoes for Bubur Cha Cha doesn't have to be cut so precisely to reduce wastage. This relaxation makes a lot of sense for an everyday version of a special festive dish.*

For the same reason, the expensive Pisang Raja banana was left out of Bubur Cha Cha. Likewise, sugar was used instead of gula Melaka, *resulting in a thinner sauce. So, Bubur Cha Cha has boiled black-eyed beans and more recently, sago, as well as the colourful* cha cha, *the jelly made from boiled starch.*

Cha cha means 'little gems' in Kristang, the Portuguese Eurasian language. It is the star item in Bubur Cha Cha. In fact, the original Malay version of Bubur Cha Cha consists only of these multi-coloured jelly.

Kolak Sari-Sari from Indonesia and the Filipino Ginataang Halo Halo are similar to Bubur Cha Cha except that they used glutinous rice balls instead of our cha cha. *The latter also includes jackfruit. In Macau, there is a sweet broth call Cha Cha made of coconut, yam, sago and green beans.*

Bubur Cha Cha

SERVES 12

120 g black-eyed beans
2 coconuts, grated
    OR 440 ml coconut milk
1 litre water to make thin
    coconut milk

450 g sweet potatoes
300 g yam
200 g sugar
1 tsp salt
6 pandan leaves, knotted
1 tbsp tapioca flour

Cha Cha Jelly
100 g tapioca flour plus
    more tapioca flour for
    dusting
1 tsp caster sugar
¼ tsp lye water (*kee chooi*)
100 ml boiling water
    (not all will be used)
5 drops each of red and
    green food colouring
50 g sugar, dissolved in
    200 ml warm water for
    soaking the jelly

Soak the black-eyed beans in water for about 2 hours. Then boil the beans in water. Simmer for about 20 minutes till the beans are just soft. Drain and set the beans aside.

Put the grated coconut in a muslin bag and squeeze to obtain the first squeeze or thick coconut milk.

Add 500 ml water to the squeezed grated coconut and mix thoroughly. Squeeze this to obtain the second squeeze coconut milk. Repeat with the remaining water. This is the thin coconut milk or *santan boey* in Penang Hokkien.

Alternatively, buy 440 ml thick coconut milk and dilute 50 ml of it in water to make up 1 litre of thin coconut milk.

Peel the skin off the sweet potatoes. Cut the flesh into slices about 1.5 cm thick, then into strips of 1.5 cm, and finally slice the strips diagonally into diamond shapes with sides of about 3 cm. Keep under water to prevent it from turning grey.

Choose yam that is lighter in weight, thus of low density, and has lots of red veins inside. Trim off the parts which are not powdery, especially the top and the bottom. Do not soak the cut yam in water. Keep the yam dry otherwise it will be difficult to handle. Peel the skin off the yam. Cuts into slices about 1.5 cm, then into strips of 1.5 cm, and finally slice the strips diagonally into diamond shapes with sides of about 3 cm. Keep the cut yam aside.

You could steam the sweet potatoes and the yam, but it is more convenient to boil them separately. Bring a pot of water with the yam to a boil, and simmer for about 8 minutes. Cook till the yam is just cooked, but not too soft because it will simmer in the coconut sauce later. Use a fork to check for doneness. Drain and keep aside the cooked yam.

Repeat with the sweet potatoes. Note that different

varieties of sweet potato and yam will have different cooking times. That is why different varieties of sweet potatoes should be boiled or steamed separately.

Cha Cha Jelly
Mix 100 g of tapioca flour with the caster sugar in a bowl and drizzle about ⅓ of the boiling water and lye water on the mixture, stirring continuously. When the water has been absorbed, drizzle more water to form a more homogenous mixture. Dust a worktop with extra tapioca flour. Remove the dough from the bowl and knead till it doesn't stick to the worktop. Add a drizzle of water, if required.

Divide the dough into three equal parts. Keep your worktop well dusted with tapioca flour. Take one portion of the dough and flatten it, then spread 4 or 5 drops of red colouring on it. Fold the dough over and knead the dough till the colour is uniformly mixed through. Divide this red dough into two portions and roll each into a rope about 1 cm in diameter. Use a knife or scissors to cut at a slant into triangular pillows. Dust the pillows with tapioca flour to prevent them from sticking together. Flatten each pillow between you finger and thumb; less puffy *cha cha* jelly will not be so chewy, especially if eaten cold.

Repeat, using the green colouring, for the second portion of the dough. Then do the same for the third white portion, without any colouring.

Boil a pot of water. When the water has boiled, put the white *cha cha* into the pot. The *cha cha* jelly will float when it is cooked. Scoop up the cooked *cha cha* with a small seive and plunge them in cold water. Do the same with the red *cha cha*, and repeat for the green *cha cha*. Keep them aside. You may need to stir the *cha cha* occasionally to prevent them from sticking together.

Drain all the *cha cha* jellies and transfer them to the prepared sugar solution. Note that the outside of the *cha cha* turns more transparent the longer it is soaked in liquid.

Assembly

Put the thin coconut milk, sugar, salt and knotted pandan leaves in a pot and bring to a boil. Then add black-eyed beans, the sweet potatoes and the yam. Bring to a boil again.

Render the tapioca flour with 2 tablespoons of water and stir this into the pot of Bubur Cha Cha to thicken the sauce. Turn off the heat.

Stir in the *cha cha* jelly and the syrup, then add the thick coconut milk. Stir well on a low heat and simmer for about 5 minutes. Do not allow it to boil or else the coconut milk may curdle.

Remove the pandan leaves before serving. Bubur Cha Cha can be served hot or chilled, but it should not be served with ice as that will dilute the sauce.

Cheak Bee Soh VEGETABLE PUFFS

Is it Cheak Bee Soh or is it Chai Bee Soh? Chai *could refer to the vegetable filling for this savory* kuih. *According to* jee chim, *my wife's aunt, it should be Cheak Bee Soh; the* cheak *refering to the main ingredient of the dough – the rice for everyday meals, which we call* cheak bee *in Hokkien, rather than* chooi bee, *the broken, unpolished rice which we fed to chickens we reared years ago in the backyard, or glutinous rice,* choo bee.

Cheak Bee Soh is virtually unknown today. Jee chim *supervised our cooking of Cheak Bee Soh nearly ten years ago. She had not cooked it for years. The last time was when she demonstrated it some ten years earlier to my wife who wrote down the recipe.*

Cheak Bee Soh looks like a crescent-shaped curry puff and this is where the similarity ends. The filling is similar to that of Koay Pai Ti, much like the traditional Epok-Epok filling of yesteryear. (The filling used in Epok-Epok in recent times is similar to that of Curry Puff, which is potato based.)

However, the pastry is quite different from that of Epok-Epok which uses wheat flour. Two different types of rice flours – cheak bee *and* choo bee *– are used to make Cheak Bee Soh pastry. The dough and the filling most probably have Hokkien origins like Poh Piah, Koay Pai Ti, and Ju Hu Char. These were originally all based on bamboo shoot. According to* jee chim, *we can add crab meat and roe to give the Cheak Bee Soh filling a dark orange colour and richer taste.*

Cheak Bee Soh used to be served at the weddings of rich families in Penang. In the 1960s, while the Nonya kuihs *like Kuih Bengka Ubi Kayu, Kuih Lapis and Chai Tow Kuih cost 5 cents each, and Curry Puffs cost 10 cents, Cheak Bee Soh cost 20 cents.*

Cheak Bee Soh

MAKES 30

Filling
225 g yambean (*bangkwang* or jicama)
75 g carrots, as a substitute for crab roe
75 g French beans
150 g prawns
150 g belly pork
100 g firm tofu (*tau kwa*)
3 cloves garlic
50 g bamboo shoots (optional), reduce yambean by 50 g if used
100 g crab meat and roe (optional)

Pastry
225 g rice flour plus extra for dusting the worktop
80 g glutinous rice flour
230 ml water
3 tbsps lard, made from about 100 g pork fat

Filling
Cut the yambean, and carrots, if using, into fine strips of about 2–3 cm long, or shred using a mandoline. Sliced the French beans thinly on the slant.

Peel the prawns, devein and dice.

Boil the prawn shells and heads with the belly pork and simmer for about half an hour. Discard the prawn shells and heads. Keep the stock for use later.

Remove the fat and skin from the belly pork. Slice the pork thinly, about 2 mm, and then cut the slices into thin strips of 2 mm wide.

Slice the firm tofu into pieces of about 2 mm thickness, and then cut into strips of 2 mm wide. Fry the tofu strips in hot oil until light brown. Drain the oil and keep the tofu aside.

Smash and chop up the garlic and fry in oil till nearly brown.

Put in the prawns and salt to taste, and fry till the prawns change from transparent to white or pink.

Add the pork strips and fry till some lard comes off the pork.

Include the carrots, if using, and fry for about 5 minutes. Include the yambean and the bamboo shoots, if using, and fry for another 5 minutes. Now add the French beans and fry till it changes from light green to dark green. Finally, add the fried firm tofu and the crab meat, if using.

Small amounts of stock could be added during the frying if the mixture is too dry. If too much stock is added, the mixture will become soggy. The aim is to fry the vegetables till they are just cooked yet crunchy.

Pastry

Mix both the rice flours with the 230 ml of water to obtain a consistent dough. Divide into four portions. Fashion each portion into a flat doughnut shape with a hole in the middle.

Boil sufficient water in a wok for boiling the four portions of dough. When the water has boiled, slip in all the dough. The dough is ready when they float to the surface.

Dust the worktop and the dough with the extra rice flour. Knead all the pieces together with the lard while still hot for about 15 minutes until the dough does not stick so much to your hands.

Assembly

Dust the worktop with rice flour, then roll out the dough to a thickness of about 1 mm. Cut into circles of about 8 to 10 cm using a small bowl or plate as a template. Dust with the rice flour regularly to prevent the dough from sticking.

Spread some crab roe, if using, on half of the pastry. Top with the filling, fold over the pastry, and press the two sides together to seal the edges as for Curry Puff. Starting from one side, pinch the edge and twist, repeating along the edge until the sealed edge looks like twisted rope. Repeat for the remaining pastry and filling.

Heat up oil for deep frying and fry batches of the Cheak Bee Soh on low heat. Remove from the oil before they turn brown. Place on kitchen paper to absorb the oil.

The Cheak Bee Soh should be crispy if the pastry is not too thick. Serve with Suan Yong Chor, the Nonya sweet, sour and spicy sauce. Alternatively, serve with a blend of bottled sweet chillie sauce, vinegar and light soya sauce.

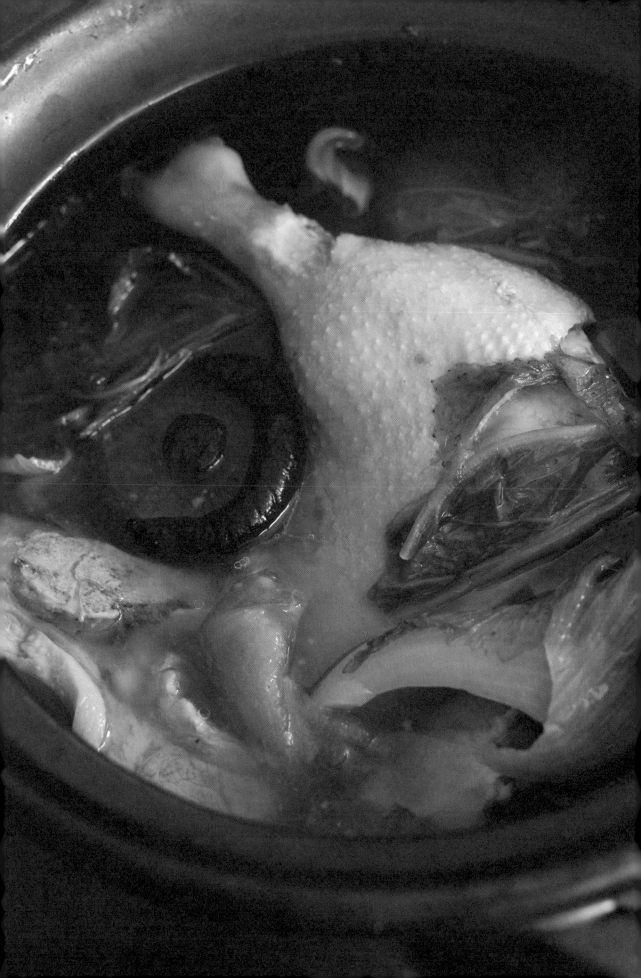

Kiam Chai Ark SALTED GREENS AND DUCK SOUP

This slightly sour Nonya soup of Chinese origin features kiam chai *and* ark *which are salted mustard greens and duck respectively in Hokkien. In Singapore and Malacca, it is known as Itek Tim,* itek *is 'duck' in Malay and in the Southern Nonya patois and* tim *means 'steam' in Hokkien. Kiam Chai Ark or Itek Tim is one of the Nonya dishes that has more similarities than difference among the versions from Singapore, Penang and Malacca. There is a Cantonese soup of salted mustard greens and duck which is steamed.*

The main ingredients of this soup, besides the obvious kiam chai *and duck, are the wet variety of sour plum and/or assam gelugor and sometimes, garlic and tomatoes. Pig trotters or pork ribs is added to give it additional flavour. For a* halal *version, leg of lamb can be substituted. The Northern Nonyas from Penang add onions, dried mushroom, nutmeg, peppercorns and whole pieces of sugarcane, whilst the Southern Nonyas add galangal, ginger, brandy and even sea cucumber. The use of brandy for this soup could well be due to the Portuguese influence in Malacca. I understand this soup also features in Eurasian cuisine.*

Traditionally, the Nonyas also add pickled watermelon skin to this soup. The white part of the watermelon skin is cut into slices and pickled in salt and fermented soya beans. My cousin Sandy says that it should be pickled for several months.

Kim Chai Ark is one of the Nonya soups served during festive events like Chinese New Year, weddings, birthdays, and as an offering at Cheng Beng and the death anniversaries of family members. The beauty of this soup is that it can keep well for several days, so it is a very handy dish for Chinese New Year, when we are not allowed to cook on the first day. Whatever remains of the Kim Chai Ark in the next few days will be turned into Kiam Chai Boey by including other left-over food like Ju Hu Char and roast duck.

In our family, Kim Chai Ark has always been cooked using a large enamel port over a Japanese charcoal stove. We use two types of kiam chai *– the yellowish-green one with the thicker stems and leaves, commonly referred to as* tng snua *(China)* kiam chai *and the local darker green* kiam chai *which has long leaves and stems. We use more of the thicker one.*

The cooking normally starts in the late afternoon. The pork is added when the water is boiling hot. The duck is put in when the soup is boiling vigourously again. The other ingredients are included when it comes to the boil again. After the soup has boiled for about another 10 minutes, the air ventilator for the stove is partially closed to reduce the heat of the charcoal fire. The pot, with the cover secured, is left overnight to simmer until the charcoal fire dies out. The soup is ready for serving the next morning.

Nowadays, salted mustard greens are found outside of Southeast Asia. It is more readily available in Chinese or Vietnamese stores, packed in sealed plastic bags or in tins. Sour plums bottled with juice can also be found in these stores. Dry salted plums can be used although it is a poor substitute.

Kiam Chai Ark

400 g thick salted mustard
  greens
100 g leafy salted mustard
  greens
200 g onions
10 cm sugarcane stem
  (optional)
10 dried shitake mushrooms
1 kg leg of pork or leg of
  lamb
1 duck, cut into four
6 sour plums
1 tbsp peppercorn
2 nutmeg seeds, shells
  broken
150 g tomatoes (optional)

Wash the thick salted mustard greens. Soak in water and squeeze out the water; repeat to remove the salt from the mustard greens. Then cut off the larger leaves from the stem. For the leafy salted mustard greens, cut the leaves into three. Leave aside.

Peel the onions, wash and cut each onion into four.

Wash and smash the sugarcane, if using.

Cut off and discard the mushroom stems. Soak the mushrooms caps in water to soften. Leave aside.

Boil 4 litres of water – sufficient to cover both the meat and the duck – in a large stock pot. Add the meat when the water has boiled. Cover the pot and, when the content is boiling, add the duck and stir well. Now include both types of mustard greens, onions, mushrooms, sour plums, nutmeg seeds, peppercorns and tomatoes.

Let it boil on medium heat for about 15 minutes, then turn the heat to low to simmer for about 2 hours. Cover the pot and leave to stand overnight. Bring to a boil the next day before serving.

In the days before refrigerators, when large amounts of food had to be stored over one or two days, we were always told to heat up soup or left-over food, cover it up properly and not to touch it until it was ready to be heated up again and served. Stirring with a used utensil was banned as it could contaminate the food. You might say that these traditional practices in the handling and storing of cooked food are the precursor of Hazard Analysis and Critical Control Points (HACCP), the modern commercial preventative food safety system for handling food

AN ENAMEL DOUBLE BOILER.

Double-Boiled Chicken Soup

It is said that chicken soup prepared in a double boiler is more nutritious than that boiled in a normal pot. I am sure that the belief is well founded, since the temperature in the top pot of the double boiler is around the boiling point of water which is 100°C. Hence, all the goodness in the chicken and the soup is preserved. Brewing the soup in a normal pot would mean that the nutrients in the ingredients would be destroyed by the higher temperature, especially if salt is added.

Commercial essence of chicken, which comes in little bottles, is said to have the same nutrition properties but our family never likes its taste. Not only that, it is quite expensive! I prefer a homemade double-boiled chicken soup anytime. Also, double-boiled chicken soup is quite easy to prepare so I tend to prepare all my chicken soups this way. The ingredients are just pieces of cut chicken and whole peppercorns.

Double boilers are also used for brewing bird's nest soup, other traditional herbal soups and for cooking Kaya.

1 chicken, about 1.2 kg
20 white peppercorns
Water
Salt to taste

Rinse the chicken and cut it into pieces. Traditionally, the chicken wing is cut into three parts, and the leg into the drumstick and thigh sections. The rest of the chicken is cut into smaller serving pieces, especially the breast, depending on family preferences.

Boil a kettle of water.

Pour in an amount of water in the lower pot of the double boiler so that when the top pot is placed over it the water doesn't overflow. Place over a fire to bring to a boil. Now, place the top pot over the bottom one and fill the top pot with the chicken pieces and the whole peppercorns. Add boiling water to cover the chicken pieces by about 3 cm. Put the cover on.

Once the water in both pots is boiling, reduce the heat so that steam is not escaping from the bottom pot and the soup is simmering away. Let the soup simmer for about another hour.

Add salt to taste, and serve.

Steamboat

Steamboat, ean lor *in Penang Hokkien, or Mongolian Hot Pot is traditionally served for dinner on Chinese New Year's Eve. The Mongolian name suggests its origin, where it is served with beef, mutton or horse meat. There are variations in the ingredients and stock in different regions of China and Southeast Asia.*

The steamboat that I grew up with offered an assortment of sliced meat, seafood, vegetable, mushroom, re-constituted dried cuttlefish, noodles, egg, meatball, prawnball and fishball. I remember that the strong-tasting tang oh (Garland Chrysanthemum) *was always included. These ingredients were arranged in plates around the steamboat. In more recent times, exotic ingredients such as abalone, scallop, sea cucumber and fish maw were introduced. Of course, other ingredients can be added according to personal preferences. Noodles are normally taken towards the end of the meal if the diners are still hungry!*

My mother used to make her own meatballs; homemade ones are much better. The recipe for meatballs is included here. Traditionally, meatballs are made of pork, but other meat can be used.

Steamboat starts with waiting for the stock to boil. We then add a portion of the ingredients to the steamboat. The cover is closed to allow the ingredients to cook. When the soup begins to boil, the cover is removed and the diners help themselves to the cooked ingredients as well as the soup. Small wire sieves are used to fish out the items from the steamboat.

When the diners have had their share of food, the steamboat is re-filled with stock and the process is repeated but at a more leisurely pace. For those who like poached or boiled eggs, it is customary to place a few leaves of lettuce in the steamboat to form a cup and then to break an egg into it. Ingredients that cook quickly, like prawns and sliced fish, need to be monitored so that they are not overcooked. Diners could add various noodles like Hokkien mee, tung hoon *(glass noodles),* bee hoon *and, more recently,* ramen.

It is best to take your time over a steamboat dinner because the soup will become more and more tasty as the food is cooked. Thus, a good stock is the most important part of the steamboat. It is prepared by boiling meat bones and simmering for several hours. I have seen all sorts of unconventional stocks used for steamboats in recent times: Fish, mushroom and herbal broth, Bak Kut Teh, thin laksa gravy, chicken curry, even thin rice porridge. In a steamboat dinner, the stock would have to be refilled four or five times depending on the number of diners.

Several dipping sauces are served with steamboat. These include sliced shallots and chopped garlic served on their own or in the oil they have been fried in, light soya sauce, and chilli sauce. Satay sauce is a more recent condiment.

The traditional steamboat is made of copper or brass and heated with charcoal embers. Food cooked in metal steamboats over coals have a special taste. Unfortunately, steamboat making is a dying trade and it is hard to find copper ones. Today, cast-aluminium steamboats and a wide variety of electrical steamboats are available.

Steamboat

SERVES 10

Stock

2 kg meat or chicken bones
5 litres water

Condiments

6 cloves garlic
8 tbsps oil
10 shallots
Light soya sauce
Bottled chilli sauce of your
  choice

Meatballs

150 g prawns, shelled and
  deveined
150 g minced meat
2 cloves garlic, finely
  chopped up
1 tbsp cornflour or tapioca
  flour
¼ tsp ground pepper
½ tsp salt
1 tbsp sesame oil
2 tbsps light soya sauce

Meats

300 g meat, thinly sliced
300 g chicken, deboned
  and thinly sliced
300 g prawns, shelled and
  deveined
300 g fish fillet, thinly sliced
Meatballs, prepared earlier
300 g fishballs

300 g fresh mushrooms, cut
  into half or quarters
300 g soft tofu, cut into
  2-cm pieces
6 eggs

Stock

To prepare the stock, boil the water and then add the bones. Turn down the heat when the stock boils again. Allow to simmer for at least 90 minutes. The stock should be kept simmering while the steamboat dinner is being served so that it is ready to top up the steamboat.

Condiments

Smash up the 6 cloves of garlic, remove the skin and chop the garlic finely. Heat up a pan, then add 4 tablespoons of oil. When the oil is hot, add the garlic. Stir continuously and, when the garlic turns slightly yellow, turn off the heat but continue stirring. The fried garlic can be served with or without the oil.

Remove the skin from the shallots and slice thinly to a uniform thickness. Heat up a pan, then add 4 tablespoons of oil. Put in the shallots when the oil is hot. Stir continuously. When the shallots turns slightly golden, turn off the heat but continue to stir. The fried shallot can be served with the oil or separately.

Meatballs

Chop up the deveined prawns. Mix the minced garlic, cornflour, ground pepper, salt, sesame oil and the light soya sauce with the minced pork and the chopped prawns.

Divide into portions to fashion into balls about 2 cm in diameter. Arrange them on a serving plate.

Meats

The meats are cut into slices about 3 mm thick, whilst the fish is sliced a bit thicker – about 5 mm. Arrange the meat, chicken, prawn, fish, meatballs and fishballs separately on individual plates.

Put the mushrooms and tofu on separate plates.

500 g cabbage

500 g Nappa cabbage

500 g garland crysanthemum (*tang oh*)

500 g green or romain lettuce

Noodles

300 g thick yellow noodles (Hokkien *mee*) blanched

200 g glass vermicelli (*tung hoon*), blanched

200 g rice vermicelli (*bee hoon*), blanched

Break the cabbage into individual leaves, remove the middle stalks and cut them into 4-cm squares. Blanch leaves and stems in boiling water and arrange on a plate ready for serving.

Chop up the Nappa cabbage into 2-cm slices and arrange on a plate ready for serving.

Separate the leaves of the *tang oh* and the lettuce and arrange them separately on individual plates ready for serving.

Separately blanch the Hokkien noodles, glass vermicelli and the rice vermicelli, and serve them in their own bowls.

Use small bowls to serve the condiments.

If a charcoal steamboat is used, start the fire in advance, filling the steamboat with the stock to less than three quarter level. Put in the ingredients which take longer to cook, like the cabbage and mushrooms. Cover, and stoke up the fire using a fan. Wait for it to boil, then add the meat and the meatballs, and cover again. When the soup comes to a boil, add the fish and the prawns which should not be overcooked.

The steamboat is ready to serve!

To cook an egg, place a piece or two of lettuce leaves in the steamboat and break the egg over the leaves. Keep a watch over it or it will be lost in the steamboat.

Refill the steamboat with the simmering stock when required.

OVERLEAF: MY MOTHER, SEATED EXTREME RIGHT, WITH RELATIVES AND FRIENDS ENJOYING A STEAMBOAT DINNER.

METAL AND WOODEN MOULDS

Nonya *kuih*s use an assortment of moulds for their preparation, some made of metal and others of wood. These moulds originate from different parts of the world; some are local to the Malayan peninsula but many have origins in China, India, Thailand, Japan, and even Europe. Most evolved in various parts of Southeast Asia, hence the regional differences.

The Koay Pai Ti mould makes deep-fried cups for this Nonya *hors d'oevre*. A whole assortment of funnels for making Roti Jala have evolved over the years. Similarly, the cast iron waffle irons for the Dutch Knieperties have become the press for Kuih Kapit which we have in Penang, Malacca, Singapore and Indonesia today. The brass Ban Chien Koay moulds haven't changed much over the years; more recent cast iron models have appeared probably due to the higher cost of copper. The designs for the individual Kuih Bahulu moulds are interesting. They reflect their Malay and Chinese origins, although there are theories that the cake has Portuguese, Dutch or even Japanese connections.

Apong Bokwa moulds and the sieve used for making *cendol* and *bee tai bak* are also featured in this section.

Besides these metal moulds, equipment made of wood are included. There are the intricately carved Ang Koo and Kuih Bangkit moulds and the Pulut Taitai box. Details of the *bee hoon*, *muruku* and Putu Mayam presses are likewise described.

Koay Pai Ti Mould

Koay Pai Ti, the attractive Nonya *hors d'oevre*, are dainty, crispy cups of deep-fried batter filled with finely shredded vegetables, meat and various garnishes. The cups are formed

BRASS KUIH BAHULU PANS.

by a fluted mould at the end of a long handle.

Pai Ti cups are made by first heating the mould in hot oil before dipping it into a batter. The batter-coated mould is then returned to the hot oil. The cup is dislodged from the mould when it holds its shape and is removed from the oil when golden brown.

The Pai Ti moulds that I am used to are made of solid brass. In the 1950s, my father had to specially commission a local blacksmith to make moulds for my mother when she first conducted her Pai Ti cooking demonstration at the YWCA in Penang. In those days, Pai Ti moulds were not readily available. Although there is now only one company in Malaysia that makes these moulds, they can be quite easily bought from sundry shops in Malaysia and Singapore. They are even available from online stores.

I have a collection of Pai Ti moulds, including a small, aluminium one from my mother-in-law which makes thumb-sized cups. I also have a twin-headed mould which would require greater dexterity and a bigger pot of oil to use.

Another mould I have is fashioned from a flat sheet of metal instead of solid brass. This is for making Kratong Thong, which literally means 'golden cups' or 'golden baskets', a Thai *hors d'oevre* similar to Pai Ti. The Thais have different fillings for this snack, including one of minced meat and diced onions, potatoes and carrots, similar to the filling used in the Javanese Kwei Patti or Kroket Tjanker and the Min Chee of Penang. I first made the connection when my wife's Aunty Jane mentioned that she used Min Chee filling in the Pai Ti cups we made for her. Besides the single ones, I have seen Kratong Thong moulds with two or four cups.

Roti Jala Funnels

Roti Jala is a lacy crepe made by drizzling batter from funnels onto a hot pan.

I was told that, in the past, ladies dipped their hands in the batter and let it drip down their fingers to drizzle the batter onto the pan. This account is quite credible if the batter is made to the right consistency. I have not tried it myself but I am quite certain this method works.

The next innovation was probably using a banana leaf cone pinned together with a *lidi*. I have seen it used by the Indian Mamaks. The flow of the batter is a bit slow since there is only one funnel, and the stream tends to be bigger, resulting in thicker crepes.

Next, some innovative Nonya or Baba most probably went to the local tinsmith to commission a cup with a few small funnels attached. My mother's old Roti Jala cup was

DIFFERENT TYPES OF ROTI JALA CUPS AND A CONE MADE OF BANANA LEAF TO DRIZZLE BATTER ONTO A HOT PAN TO MAKE THE LACY PANCAKE.

made from galvanized iron like other household utensils in the past. Later versions were made from copper sheets.

I have a collection of Roti Jala cups of various sizes and different number of funnels. The cups with the funnels on the bottom have to be moved away from the pan while the funnels are still dripping. The improved version has the funnels on the side so that the flow of the batter can be easily controlled by tilting the cup.

Roti Jala cups, moulded cheaply in plastic, are now available. A friend was so pleased with her new plastic Roti Jala cup that she decided to throw away her old copper one. Fortunately, I heard about it in the nick of time. It was recovered from her dustbin – and that was how I acquired another old Roti Jala cup!

I have come across plastic bottles with funnels on their covers to dispense mustard or tomato sauce. These too can be used to squirt out Roti Jala batter.

Even if you cannot find any of these Roti Jala cups, all you need to do is to get a tin can and punch a few holes at the bottom. Alternatively, punch holes on the cap of any plastic drink bottle. Both work just as well!

Kuih Kapit Irons

Kuih Kapit or Love Letters is also known as Kuih Belanda and Kue Sapik in Indonesia. *Sapik* or *sepik* in Indonesian have the same meaning as *sepit* in Malay – 'to pinch, squeeze or clamp', while *kapit* in Malay means 'to press together from both sides'. These two words give a clue as to how Kuih Kapit is made. *Belanda* is 'Dutch' in Malay, clearly indicating that this waffle cookie has a Dutch origin.

The Dutch have three cookies made with waffle irons. Ijzerkoekjes is soft and oval while Knieperties, 'little pinches' in Dutch, is a sweet, thin, crispy waffle much like Kuih Kapit. Rollechies is the rolled version of Knieperties. The original Dutch waffle irons, known as *koekjesijzer*, were made of cast iron, *ijzer* being 'iron' in Dutch. The ones used to make Knieperties is very similar to Kuih Kapit moulds. Both consist of a matching pair of round moulds connected by a hinge to two long handles. When the handles are brought together, the moulds are squeezed shut.

Thus, it is clear that Knieperties were adapted in Indonesia and Malaya to become Kuih Belandah and Kuih Kapit. Along the way, the waffle became thinner. Designs of animals, birds or floral elements were etched on each mould so that the decorations were imprinted on both sides of the waffle.

The moulds used by my parent's generation were made of brass, and the truly vintage

THE PRETTY DESIGNS OF KUIH KAPIT ARE OFTEN UNAPPRECIATED BECAUSE THE WAFFLES ARE FOLDED OR ROLLED UP.

ones are of iron and copper. Now, the moulds are cast from aluminium. There are early Kuih Kapit moulds which are 30-cm square, or rectangular so that two waffles can be made at a time. The Indonesian rectangular moulds were thicker and more bulky.

To make Kuih Kapit, the iron is first heated over a slow charcoal fire. The batter is then poured on to cover completely one of the moulds before the two sides are squeezed shut and replaced over the fire. When toasted through, the Kuih Kapit is peeled off the mould and either quickly folded into quarters or rolled into a pipe. Once the waffle is cooled, it will be impossible to unfold or unroll without breaking it into pieces. This is why Kuih Kapit is also known as Love Letters.

Ban Chien Koay Pan

The small Ban Chien Koay pans, either made of brass or cast iron, are available today. Traditionally, they were made of brass. There is little difference between the two. The advantage of the cast iron pan is that it can also be used on an induction cooker that has very good temperature control and no hot surface.

To cook Ban Chien Koay, you will need an insulated glove to hold the pan firmly while you remove the pancake. This is done with a scrapper to prise the crispy Ban Chien Koay from the sides and bottom of the pan.

A cover is also needed to cover the pan as the Ban Chien Koay cooks. A wooden cover is preferred to minimise condensation.

I find that a one-egg, 12-cm pan is a good substitute for the Ban Chien Koay pan.

Kuih Bahulu Pan

Kuih Bahulu are small sponge cakes. Traditional Kuih Bahulu pans were made of brass, with individual moulds of various designs within. These designs are of the lobed Malay gooseberry (*cermai, Phyllanthus acidus*) which is sometimes described as button, egg, fish, seashell, and butterfly. There are also Chinese designs which look like vegetables and fruits with leaves. The Nonya pans have a mix of many designs while other pans have only one or two designs. The Malays favour the Malay gooseberry design.

The Kuih Bahulu pan comes in different sizes with the larger ones making twelve cakes in one baking. Each pan has a cover. When in use, the pan is heated over a charcoal stove, with burning charcoal also placed on the cover.

It is now more difficult to find brass pans since the new pans are of aluminium.

BAKING KUIH BAHULU THE TRADITIONAL WAY REQUIRES COAL IN THE OVEN AND ON THE COVER OF THE CAKE PAN.

Chinese confectionery shops sell what Hokkiens call Kuih Polu. The old pans for these cakes were made of copper and were oval or a rounded triangle. Kuih Polu are much larger than the Nonya and Malay Kuih Bahulu.

Traditionally, the Malays use Kuih Bahulu pans with egg-shaped moulds for Kuih Cara, a cake different from Kuih Bahulu. There is an egg-shaped waffle similar to Kuih Bahulu that is popular in Hong Kong called Kai Tan Chai, literally 'little eggs'.

Kay Nooi Koe also means 'egg cakes'. I remember that there was a crispy version and a steamed version. These were made with waffle irons with the shapes of chicks or fishes on both the top and bottom.

Apong Bokwa/Balek Mould

Like most traditional moulds, Apong Bokwa moulds were made of brass. Today, most of the moulds sold are made of aluminium. The same mould could also be used for making Penang Apong Balek. My understanding is that the versions of Apong Balek from Malacca and Singapore doesn't use any special moulds

Cendol Sieve

Both *cendol* and *bee tai bak* were prepared using a sieve consisting of a frame and a metal sheet with numerous holes punched through.

The name *bee tai bak* explains it all: *bee* means 'rice' in Hokkien, *tai* means 'sieve' and *bak* means 'eye', referring to the holes in the sieve.

Ground rice is the main ingredient of *bee tai bak*. The dough is first kneaded, and then water is added to form a paste which is wiped over the sieve to form the short noodles which are cooked when they fall into the boiling water placed below. *Cendol* is similarly prepared. Nonyas make ground green bean (*lek tau hoon*) into a paste. It is then pressed through the sieve to form the short, green noodles that are caught in a basin of ice water.

Cendol and *bee tai bak* are used in desserts, but the latter is also used in savoury dishes.

Ang Koo Moulds

Wooden Ang Koo moulds are skillfully carved individually for different sizes and shapes of the cake. The common shapes are that of a tortoise, a peach and a Chinese gold bar. If you look at the design of the tortoise carefully, you will see its head, tail and four feet.

A WELL-USED SMALL, VINTAGE ANG KOO MOULD.

You can still buy the all-in-one wooden mould with the shape of a tortoise on one side and the shape of a peach on the opposite side. A small version of the tortoise and the peach are carved together on the third side, while the gold bar is carved on the fourth.

In the past, brass Ang Koo moulds were also used. Today, they are also available in plastic.

Kuih Bangkit Moulds

Wooden Kuih Bangkit moulds are used by the Nonyas, especially in Penang, while pastry cutters are used by both Malays and Nonyas to make Kuih Bangkit. Some Nonyas use a pair of pincers to form patterns on the cookie if pastry cutters are used.

The wooden moulds of floral and animal shapes are washed and left to dry thoroughly before use. A dusting of flour helps to remove the cookie from the mould when it is done.

Pulut Taitai Box

A specially made wooden box was used to compress steamed glutinous rice for Pulut Taitai. As *tekan* is the Malay word for 'compress', this *kuih* is also known as Pulut Tekan.

The box consists of a base with an elevated platform, a detachable open box without a base or top, and a cover which fits in the open box so that the cover can be pushed downwards to compress the steamed rice.

The open box is placed on the base and the box is lined with banana leaves with sufficient overhang to eventually cover the rice. The blue and white steamed rice is put in the box and spread evenly. When all the rice has been placed in the box, the banana leaves are folded over to cover the rice. The cover is then carefully placed in the box and pressure is applied on the cover to compress the rice. A heavy weight like a *lesong* or a *batu giling* is put on the cover to maintain the pressure for about 8 hours to obtain the correct texture for the rice so that it will not break up when cut. In the old days, it was not uncommon for a man to stand on the cover. My classmate told me that her father carried her to increase the pressure!

Pulut Taitai is normally prepared late in the day and left overnight so that the rice becomes less sticky and easier to cut. A slab of Pulut Taitai sits on the base, ready to be cut, when you remove the cover and box.

My cousin Sandy showed me how to prepare this *kuih* using the original box belonging to her mother and my *tua kor* – most senior aunt – the late Ong Kim Inn. The box was very well made using hardwood and dovetail joints.

MIXING THE BLUE AND WHITE GLUTINOUS RICE IN A PULUT TAITAI BOX.

I made a sketch of the box and adjusted the internal dimensions to 6 in x 12 in to make 1 kg of Pulut Taitai. I also made sure that my foot could fit the cover should there be a need to stand on it! With the plan in hand, I went to a timber yard in Penang. The long wait to talk to the boss paid off because, although I only wanted him to cut the timber to the specified sizes, to my pleasant surprise, he offered to make the box for me! He told me that he had made one for his mother many years ago. It was not plain sailing though. It was many months and several visits to the timber yard before I got my Pulut Taitai box. It was well made. We settled for stainless steel screws; I didn't want to push my luck by asking for dovetail joints.

If you do not have a Pulut Taitai box, use two cake tins with detachable bases. You use the second base as a cover to press down the steamed rice.

Press for Bee Hoon, Putu Mayam and Muruku

Bee hoon is rice vermicelli, Putu Mayam are nests of fine, rice vermicelli popular in Southern India, and *muruku* are crunchy, savoury Indian snacks.

Bee hoon, Putu Mayam and *muruku* are all made using a press with two parts. One part is made from a solid piece of wood with a handle on either side of a cylindrical hole which can fit a brass disc at the bottom. You can choose from brass discs with holes of different sizes for the extrusion of dough to make noodles of various thickness – bigger holes for the coarse *bee hoon* used for Laksa, smaller ones for fine *bee hoon* and Putu Mayam, and other profiles and sizes for the assortment of *muruku*.

The second part of the press is a cylindrical block with two handles that matches the first part. The cylindrical block fits nicely into the hole, allowing it to press the dough through the holes of the brass disc. Both hands are needed to bring the handles together to squeeze the dough out.

When my grandmother made Laksa, she also made the *bee hoon* or Laksa *bor*. The dough she used is made mainly of ground rice. Some other flour like green bean or tapioca flour is added to make the *bee hoon* more *al dente*. A *bee hoon* press is filled with dough and squeezed so that the noodles fall into a pot of boiling water.

The *bee hoon* press and the smaller Putu Mayam press (known as *sevanazhi*) are remarkably alike which suggest that they have similar origins, most probably Chinese. The adoption by the Tamils and Southern Indians probably occurred centuries ago in view of the historical trade links between the two regions. For Putu Mayam, unlike *bee hoon*, the extruded vermicelli is spread over a bamboo rack and steamed. The *muruku* press I use is made from rubber wood with an assortment of plastic extrusion discs.

BEE HOON, PUTU MAYAM AND MURUKU PRESSES WITH EXTRUSION DISCS OF VARIOUS GAUGES AND DESIGNS.

Ang Koo GLUTINOUS RICE CAKE WITH BEAN FILLING

Ang Koo is also known as Ang Koo Koay. Koay in Chinese happens to have the same meaning as kuih *in Malay and* kue *in Indonesian. A* koay, kuih, *or* kue *is a sweet or savoury dessert, snack, confectionery, cake, patty, dumpling, biscuit or cookie.*

Ang Koo which means 'red tortoise' in Hokkien, is made from a filling of green bean paste wrapped in a thin sheet of glutinous rice dough coloured red. The dough is pressed into a wooden mould to form the shape of a tortoise shell. It is placed over a small piece of banana leaf and steamed. The tortoise is the symbol of longevity and prosperity. Red is an auspicious colour in Chinese culture which symbolises good fortune and joy.

Ang Koo Koay is especially prepared and used as ritual offerings for Chinese festivals such as Cheng Beng (All Souls Day) and Chinese New Year, for auspicious occasions such as baby's first month, birthdays, weddings, and also for solemn events like death anniversaries and wakes. For the latter, black Ang Koo is prepared. The Hokkiens prepare Ang Koo shaped like a long Chinese-style gold bar for the birthday of the Jade Emperor (pai thnee kong).

Ang Koo is now sold throughout the year with other Nonya kuihs, and in different colours, mainly to distinguish the different varieties of fillings used within the dough. Traditional fillings include pounded peanuts with sesame seeds; less traditional fillings include grated coconut cooked with gula Melaka *known as* inti *in Malay, red bean, yam and sesame pastes and durian.*

The Ang Koo features prominently in the Nonya muah guay *or baby's first month celebrations, when Nasi Kunyit with chicken curry and red boiled eggs are distributed to friends and relatives. Each of these items – rice, meat and egg – has a symbolic meaning. If the baby is a boy, in addition to the normal shaped ones, there will be round Ang Koo. For a girl, there will be peach-shaped Ang Koo. You can work out which parts of the anatomy the shapes refer to!*

The muah guay *celebrated by the Babas and the Nonyas is a good example of how Baba culture is a marriage between Malay and Chinese cultures. Nasi Kunyit and chicken curry have Malay origins. The practice of giving away red boiled eggs is prevalent among both the Chinese and the Malays.*

Traditional Ang Koo dough is made from ground glutinous rice only, but, in more recent times, boiled or steamed sweet potato has been added so that the dough remain soft, long after it has been steamed. In my youth, Ang Koo made the day before were fried with a little oil, flattened with a spatula and served when brown and crispy – a different texture from the fresh Ang Koo.

The colour of the Ang Koo is determined by the sweet potato used without resorting to artificial colouring. We have more choices of colours of sweet potatoes today – white, yellow, orange and purple. For green Ang Koo, use colouring extracted from pandan leaves with white or yellow sweet potatoes. For black, use ground black glutinous rice. As sweet potatoes of different colours have different water content, the amount of water used must be adjusted to achieve the desired texture of the dough.

Ang Koo

Banana leaves, cut into
   pieces to fit the size and
   shape of the Ang Koo
5 tbsps oil
6 shallots

Dough
160 g sweet potatoes
3 pandan leaves
200 g glutinous rice flour
1 tbsp rice flour plus extra
   for dusting mould
100 g coconut cream or
   concentrated coconut
   milk
Pinch of salt

Filling
200 g split green beans
   without skin, soaked for
   at least 2 hours
3 pandan leaves, each tied
   into a knot
3 tbsps shallot oil
130 g sugar
½ tsp salt
220 ml water

Preparation

Cut the banana leaves into the shape but slightly larger than the base of the Ang Koo according to the mould.

Prepare a small sieve and the extra ground rice flour ready for dusting the inside of the mould.

Shallot oil will be needed for the filling as well as for brushing the Ang Koo after steaming. To prepare the shallot oil, slice the shallots thinly. Heat up the oil, then fry the sliced shallots till they are golden brown. Remove the pan from the fire. Alternatively, microwave the sliced shallot until they are golden brown. Separate the fried shallot from the oil. Use 3 tablespoons of the shallot oil for the filling and the rest for glazing the Ang Koo after steaming.

Dough

As dry ground rice is used, it is best to prepare the dough first to allow the ground rice in the dough to absorb the water. Leave the dough aside for at least one hour before use.

Peel the sweet potatoes and cut into slices of 1 cm thick. Boil with pandan leaves in a pot with more than enough water to cover the potatoes, then simmer till the potatoes are cooked. Remove the pandan leaves and drain all but 80 ml of the water.

Remove the sweet potatoes and mash and sieve them. There is no need to sieve if a food processor is used. Put the mashed potato back into the pot and add 80 ml of the reserved water.

Include the glutinous rice flour, rice flour, coconut milk, salt and blend together. Knead this dough. Add more glutinous rice flour if the dough is too wet and soft; add more water if the dough is too dry. You need a texture like that of bread dough – springy, yet holds its shape. Set aside in a plastic bag or in a covered container.

Dust the Ang Koo mould with rice flour and take a

portion of the dough to fill up the mould to make a trial Ang Koo. Use a knife to trim off any excess dough from the mould. Knock out the dough from the mould and weigh it. This is the approximate weight of each Ang Koo.

Filling
The filling can be made in advance.

Wash the green beans and soak them in water for at least 2 hours.

Rinse the beans and drain. Put 300 ml of water in a pot and include the green beans and the pandan leaves. Bring to the boil and simmer for about 20-25 minutes till the beans are soft. Discard the pandan leaves. Drain away some of the water till the boiled beans and remaining water weigh 420 gm. Blend in a food processor or mash through strainer to make the bean paste.

Heat the shallot oil, add the sugar, salt and the green bean paste and stir till smooth. Alternatively, blend in a food processor.

Divide the filling into portions, each weighing half of the weight of the trial Ang Koo. Roll each portion of the filling between your palms to make round balls. Set aside.

Assembly
Divide the dough into portions, each weighing half of the total weight of the trial Ang Koo. Roll each portion of the dough between your palms to make round balls. Set aside.

Take one portion of the dough, flatten it into a circle and wrap it round a ball of the filling prepared earlier. Gently shape the dough so that there is a uniform layer covering the filling. Then roll the filled dough between your palms to get a round form, ensuring that the surface is smooth. Place on a plate which has been well oiled.

Repeat for the rest of the dough and filling.

Start the fire to boil the water for the steamer.

Dust the inside of the Ang Koo mould with rice flour. This is to ensure that the Ang Koo will detach from the mould easily.

Fashion the filled dough into a shape closer to that of the mould and press it in. Apply some pressure to level the dough and get a good impression of the details of the mould, especially at the edge. Knock the mould on the worktop to dislodge the Ang Koo. Blow away the excess rice flour from the Ang Koo and place it over a piece of prepared oiled banana leaf. Repeat for the rest of the filled dough.

For round Ang Koo, do not use the mould. Simply place a round filled dough over a banana leaf.

Place as many of the Ang Koo as can fit on a steaming tray.

Steam for about 5-8 minutes, depending on the size of the Ang Koo. Control the heat so that there is a moderate amount of steam generated. The Ang Koo is ready when the colour changes from dull to bright. Peep to inspect without letting out too much steam. Do not over steam, otherwise the dough will expand and the patterns on the Ang Koo will be lost when the Ang Koo cools down. When opening the cover of the steamer, make sure that the condensation on the cover does not drip on the Ang Koo.

Glaze the steamed Ang Koo by brushing them with the shallot oil. The Ang Koo is ready to be served when they have cooled down.

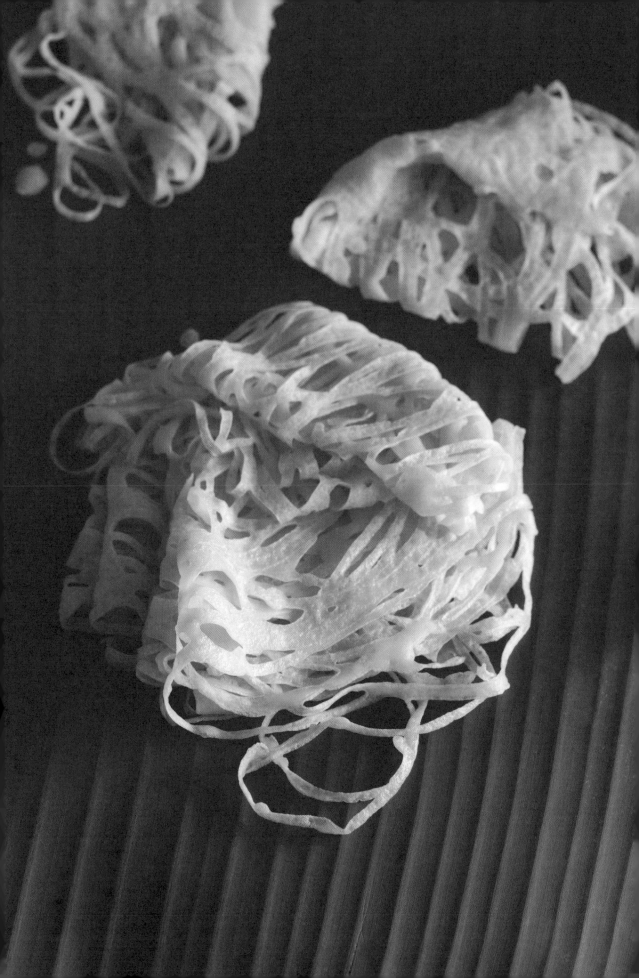

Roti Jala LACY PANCAKE

Lacy pancake is a good description for Roti Jala, a traditional Malay dish which has been adopted by the Nonyas. Roti is 'bread' and jala is 'fishing net' in Malay. So, Roti Jala could be more elegantly interpreted as Fishnet Crepe. A recipe in Female Cookbook 1981 *refers to this dish as Roti Renda,* renda *being 'lace' in Malay. Therefore, a properly made Roti Jala should look like a fishnet or lace, with fine gaps between the thin strings. I have decided that Roti Jala should be re-branded as Roti World Wide Web to keep in step with the Internet Age.*

Roti Jala batter is made by mixing flour, egg and coconut milk. It will be yellow if sufficient eggs are used, but a bit of turmeric will enhance its colour. In the old days, eggs were relatively expensive so fewer eggs were used and turmeric powder was added. Today, as we are told that turmeric is good for us, it is included in this recipe.

The basic ingredients for the batter have not changed. What has changed is the way the batter is poured on a hot frying pan to create the lacy pattern. In my distant past, I have seen Malay and Indian Mamak hawkers using banana leaves and lidi *to make a small funnel for drizzling the batter over the pan. The inventive Nonyas most probably went to Chinese metal-smiths and ordered the Roti Jala cup. It is basically a cup made of cast iron, tin or copper with three to six small funnels soldered to the bottom. There is also a more user-friendly design which has the funnels on the side to allow you to better control the flow of the batter. With advances in plastic mouldings, Roti Jala cups are now more commonly made of plastic.*

The Nonyas made everything very finely. Their beads and beadwork are fine and, in cooking, they cut and slice ingredients very meticulously and finely. This characteristic extends to making Roti Jala. The lace of the Roti Jala made by the older generation is really very fine. It looks easy, but to make it well is an art which requires practice and experience.

Take a look at the photos of Roti Jala posted on the Internet to see the wide-ranging quality. Some so-called Roti Jala look more like pancakes with holes in them!

Roti Jala is cooked on one side only, unlike crepes or pancakes which are cooked on both sides. Once cooked, it is folded into a semicircle, then into a quarter and finally into one-eighth. They are then arranged eight in a layer on a round serving dish. If they are not folded and just stacked one on top of another it would be difficult to separate a Roti Jala from the one below. This is how we prepare and serve Roti Jala in our family. Some families may fold their Roti Jala into quarters, while others roll them up.

The proper way to eat Roti Jala is to unfold each piece and have it with a generous amount of curry sauce. Hence it is easier to eat with your fingers. In our family we always eat it with Gulai Kay – Nonya chicken curry cooked Malay style or lamb curry. It can, of course, be eaten with other curries. Roti Jala can also be served as a pancake accompanied by lemon and honey or syrup.

Roti Jala is popular today for breaking fast during Ramadan (Muslim fasting month).

Roti Jala

600 g flour
½ tsp salt
½ tsp turmeric powder
6 eggs
100 ml milk or coconut milk
    squeezed from ½ coconut,
    grated
850 ml water
Oil
Paper tissue for oiling pan

Batter

Sieve the flour into a mixing bowl and add the salt and the tumeric. Using a food processor, beat the eggs, one at a time into the flour mixture. Now add the milk or coconut milk gradually, stirring to obtain a smooth, thick paste. Finally, include water a little at a time and stir well. If too much water is added at once, it will be difficult to get rid of the lumps in the batter. If the batter is still lumpy, sieve it, or the lumps would block the funnels of the Roti Jala cup.

Test the consistency of the batter through the Roti Jala cup. The batter flowing from the funnels should come out in continuous streams. If they come out in droplets, the batter is too thick. Add more water and repeat the test. If the stream is too watery, add more flour and mix well to remove the lumps. Let the batter sit for at least ½ hour before making the Roti Jala.

Making Roti Jala

Heat up a non-stick pan. Use a paper tissue to coat a thin layer of oil all over the pan.

Place the Roti Jala cup over a bowl to collect the batter that flows out through the funnels. Ladle batter into the cup till it is about half to three quarter full. Hold the bowl with one hand and the cup with the other. Move both over the pan and then move the cup over the pan, making circular or figure-of-eight patterns to from a lacy crepe of about 20 cm in diameter. The aim is to make a uniform, thin crepe. The thickness of the web is dependent on the speed which the mould is moved over the pan and on the thickness of the batter. Return the cup to the bowl once you have a lacy crepe.

The Roti Jala is ready when it separates from the pan at the edges. Lift the pan and tilt it to allow the Roti Jala to slide onto a plate. Fold the crepe into eighths. Arrange on a serving plate.

Repeat with remaining batter.

Kuih Bangkit TAPIOCA FLOUR BISCUITS

Kuih Bangkit is one of the must have cookies for the Nonya and Babas.

Although kuih *and* bangkit *are Malay words, the origin of Kuih Bangkit may not be Malay. There is a suggestion that it may be of China – an adaptation of an ancestral altar offering known as* shu fun paeng *or tapioca flour biscuit in Cantonese.*

However, the Brazilian connection is also plausible since tapioca is native to Brazil and was spread all over the world by the early Portuguese and Spanish explorers. There is a starch cookie in Brazil called Bolachinha de Goma, which is very similar to Kuih Bangkit except the shape is not the same. The ingredients used are identical: Tapioca flour, coconut milk, sugar, and egg, with the addition of a generous amount of butter. One recipe recommend drying the tapioca starch in the sun.

Baba Peter Lee's research suggests that although bangkit *means 'to rise' in Malay, it could also be* banket, *which is Dutch for 'biscuit'. There are four recipes for different types of* banket *in the book* Oost-Indisch Kookboek (East Indies Cookbook) *published in 1861. One of them, Theebanket (tea banket) is made from flour, sugar, butter and egg. The ingredients are kneaded into a dough, rolled out, cut into shapes and baked.*

A good Kuih Bangkit should only crumble and melt when placed in the mouth and it should not stick to the palate; it should be crunchy but not too hard. Therefore, the amount of water used in the recipe is key. The tapioca flour should be as dry as possible, and the coconut milk used should be as concentrated as possible. The coconut milk available commercially, in packets and in cans, have less fat and therefore has higher percentage of water. The first squeeze santan *from grated coconut is preferred. However, if you must use tinned or packaged coconut milk, some of the non-fatty liquid could be removed by letting the coconut milk stand in a tall glass so that you can use only the coconut cream on top. In temperate climates, coconut milk must be warmed up to body temperature to melt the fat in the coconut milk. Look for the brand with the highest percentage fat when buying packaged coconut milk; it should be as high as 25 percent.*

For Kuih Bangkit, the moisture in the tapioca should be removed by frying the flour over low heat, baking in an oven or using a microwave oven. The total weight of the flour should reduce by at least 10 percent. Pandan leaves are added in the process to give the flour a pandan flavour.

If wooden moulds are to be used, they should be washed and left to dry thoroughly well before use.

Tapioca flour used for Kuih Bangkit produces a white cookie. As white is considered an inauspicious colour for the Nonyas, the traditional practice is to decorate Kuih Bangkit with a red dot; for animal shapes, both eyes are dotted.

Kuih Bangkit

MAKES ABOUT 40 KUIHS OF 3-3.5 CM IN WIDTH

4 pandan leaves
200 g tapioca flour
1 egg yolk
90 g sugar
120 ml first squeeze coconut
    milk, from half a coconut,
    grated
Pinch of salt
Red food colouring
Toothpick

Wash the pandan leaves. Dry them and cut into lengths of about 2 cm.

Sieve the flour and fry it with the pandan leaves in a large wok over low heat for about 10-15 minutes. Alternatively, mix the tapioca flour with the pandan leaves and bake in an oven at 160°C for about an hour.

Leave the flour to cool and remove the pandan leaves. Sieve the flour into a large basin or container, otherwise the flour will fly all over the kitchen. Set aside about 15 g of the flour for dusting the worktop and the wooden moulds. Store the rest of the flour in a sealed container or plastic bag.

Whisk the egg yolk and the sugar togther till you get a thick and creamy mixture. Add the coconut milk and the salt, and blend together.

Mix this coconut mixture gradually with the flour to form a dough. Knead till the dough is firm. You may not need to use all the coconut mixture.

Line a baking tray with a non-stick baking sheet or grease-proof paper.

Using Wooden Moulds
Dust the moulds evenly with the flour that was set aside. Take a portion of dough and press it into the moulds. Use more than enough so that the excess dough can be sliced off with a knife to make a level bottom for the cookie. Keep the excess dough pressed together in a covered bowl.

Holding the filled mould at an angle, knock the end of the mould on a firm surface to take out the moulded dough. Place the moulded dough on the baking sheet about 1 cm apart.

Some dough may be stuck in the details of the unmoulded cookie if the mould was not dusted evenly with flour. Use a toothpick to gently pick the dough out without distorting the Kuih Bangkit.

When the portion of the dough you have taken has been used up, knead the excess dough cut from the mould with some of the dough you have set aside. Include a little of the coconut mixture and knead till the dough is firm.

Fill the moulds and repeat till all the dough has been used up.

Using Pastry Cutter
Dust the worktop and a rolling pin with the flour that has been set aside.

Take a portion of dough and roll it out to a thickness of about ½ cm. Cut the dough with a Kuih Bangkit or other small cookie cutter. Some Nonyas use a pincer to make patterns on each Kuih Bangkit. Place the cookies on the baking sheet about 1 cm apart.

Knead the trimmings of the cut dough with fresh dough, adding a little of the coconut mixture that has been set aside. Knead till you get a firm dough.

Baking
Bake in a pre-heated oven at 160°C for about 10-15 minutes till the Kuih Bangkit shows a hint of brown on the edges. Remove the tray from the oven and allow the cookies to cool.

Put the red food colouring in a small bowl and use a toothpick make a dot on each cookie.

Kuih Bangkit should be stored in an airtight container otherwise it will not remain crunchy.

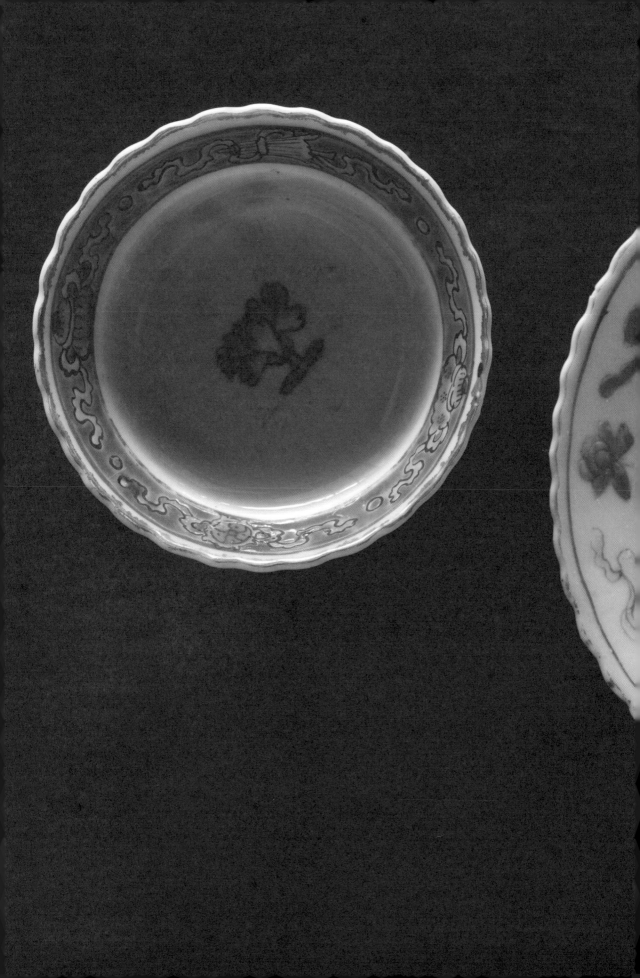

Pulut Taitai GLUTINOUS RICE WITH COCONUT AND EGG JAM

This Nonya kuih, known as Pulut Taitai in Penang, is called Pulut Tata and Pulut Tatal in Singapore, and Pulut Tekan in Malacca. Taitai, which means 'stupid' in Penang Hokkien, is probably a corruption of tartal, the thick coconut-milk-based sauce that once accompanied the pulut before it was replaced by Kaya.

Today, Kaya is spread on top of each rectangular slice of steamed glutinous rice which has a characteristic blue and white mottle effect.

The blue of the kuih comes from the indigo flower of bunga telang or Butterfly Pea (Clitoria ternatea), a creeper which was once commonly grown on the garden fences of Nonya homes. This is not the indigo of textile dying which is derived from the leaves of the plant Indigofera tinctoria.

Pulut Taitai is one of the kuihs served at Penang Nonya weddings with others like Ondeh Ondeh (page 92), Kuih Bengka Ubi Kayu (page 97) and Kow Chan Kuih (page 173).

Pulut Taitai is somewhat similar to Kuih Salat which is also known as Seri Muka and Gadang Galoh. Kuih Salat also has two layers. Although the bottom layer is compressed glutinous rice like Pulut Taitai, it is usually white and topped with a layer of green, pandan-flavoured Kaya. I prefer Pulut Taitai with Kaya; the proportion of glutinous rice and Kaya in Kuih Salat is not to my taste – too much Kaya!

For Pulut Taitai, the glutinous rice is soaked in water, steamed with coconut milk and traditionally compressed in a specially made wooden bo. The word for 'compress' in Malay is tekan, hence the Malaccan name of Pulut Tekan.

I use my custom-made Pulut Taitai box but you can use a square 18-cm square baking tin with a removable bottom plus the bottom of a similar cake tin to compress the steamed glutinous rice.

Pulut Taitai

18-cm square cake tin

Banana leaves for lining the
   cake tin
4 pandan leaves
90 dried Butterfly Pea
   flowers (*bunga telang*)

700 g glutinous rice
560 g grated coconut,
   squeezed for 280 ml first
   squeeze coconut milk
   OR 280 ml thick coconut
   milk
1½ tsp salt
1 bottle Kaya (see page 178)
   for spreading over the
   compressed glutinous rice

Clean and blanch the banana leaves. Line the bottom and sides of the cake tin with banana leaves, leaving some to line the top and to spread the rice.

Clean the pandan leaves. Tear each leaf, lengthwise, into four and tie into a knot. Set aside.

Soak the *bunga telang* in hot water, then squeeze the flowers to extract the blue colouring. Add more water and repeat till the petals are grey.

Soak just under two-thirds of the glutinous rice in the blue *bunga telang* solution for at least 4 hours.

Soak the remaining glutinous rice in plain water.

Line a steamer with cloth and put in the soaked blue rice and soaked white rice, keeping them separate. Use a chopstick to make holes in the rice to allow the steam to go through.

Steam the rice for 7 minutes, then stir each colour of rice separately to bring the rice on the bottom to the top so that the rice is uniformly steamed. Use a chopstick to make holes in the rice again. Continue steaming for 8 minutes.

Sprinkle or spray about 150 ml of water uniformly over the steamed rice, turning over each colour of rice seperately so that the rice at the bottom is also wet. Steam for another 10 minutes.

Now stir the rice, again seperately, so that the rice on the top and at the bottom of steamer is steamed uniformly. Poke holes in the rice for the steam to get through. Steam for a further 10 minutes.

Mixing the steamed rice with the santan
This process is called *aloo*. Put several large spoonfuls of the steamed blue rice in a mixing bowl and stir well.

Use a wooden spoon to spread 3 tablespoons of the thick coconut milk over it. Break up the lumps of rice so that the grains are separated. Add more thick coconut milk, if necessary, to loosen the lumps of rice. If you can see the white of the coconut milk between adjacent grains of rice, then there is too much coconut milk. If you have put in too much coconut milk, mix the rice with the next batch. Repeat for the remainder of the blue rice. Do the same for the white rice.

Put the rice back into the steamer, keeping the two colours separate. Include the knotted pandan leaves and steam.

After about 10 minutes, stir the rice, keeping the two colours separate, so that the rice on top and at bottom of steamer is uniformly steamed. Make holes in the rice for the steam to get though. Continue steaming for another 5 to 10 minutes till cooked.

Transfer the steamed blue rice into the cake tin which has been lined with banana leaves. Mix spoonfuls of white steamed rice with the blue rice to obtain a mottled effect. Do not over mix.

Ensure that the rice fills up the corners and the sides of the cake tin and that the rice is uniformly spread and tightly packed. You could use a piece of banana leaf to spread out the sticky steamed rice.

Cover the steamed rice with the banana leaves, trimming away excess banana leaves if necessary. Carefully place the bottom of another cake tin as a cover over the banana leaves and apply uniform pressure, ensuring that the cover is horizontal.

Place a heavy weight on the cover and leave overnight. Remove the weight and the cover of the cake tin. Support the removable bottom of the tin and take out the compressed steamed rice in one nice, thick block.

Slice the compressed rice into 1-cm thick slabs, and each slab into 3 equal pieces.

Spread a tablespoon or more of Kaya over each piece of the compressed steamed rice and enjoy.

Kuih Kapit LOVE LETTERS

Kuih Kapit is a very thin, crispy wafer which is one of the delicacies served by Nonyas to visitors during Chinese New Year and other festivities. Chay is the Hokkien word used to describe the texture of the Kuih Kapit which melts in the mouth; it is crispy but not too brittle.

Kuih Kapit is also known as Love Letters. Legend has it that Kuih Kapit were used by lovers to communicate covertly by rolling or folding love notes in the kuih.

Kuih Kapit is of Dutch origin. Knieperties ('little pinches' in Dutch) is a thin waffle much like Kuih Kapit. The waffle iron for Knieperties and Kuih Kapit are very similar too. Interestingly, the Dutch also served their Knieperties around the New Year. On New Year's Eve, the round Knieperties are served flat, symbolising the completely unfolded year. The rolled up wafers, also known as Rollechies, are served on New Year's Day – representing the new, still folded year ahead.

Today's Kuih Kapit are either folded into a quadrant or formed into a roll. Those from Malacca and Singapore are commonly rolled, while those from Penang are more usually folded. In certain parts of Indonesia, it is also known as Kue Semprong because the rolled version is like semprong, the Indonesian word for 'bamboo'. The Nonyas in Phuket added black sesame seeds to their Kuih Kapit batter.

I find it very interesting that there are two separate recipes for the flat Knieperties and the rolled Rollechies. Knieperties are made using a dough of flour, sugar, egg, butter, water and cinnamon. A small ball of the dough is placed in the middle of one side of the waffle iron and the two sides are squeezed together to form a flat waffle. The rolled wafer, however, is made from a batter with similar ingredients, but with the water replaced by a larger quantity of milk. This recipe is similar to that of Kuih Kapit, which uses ground rice and coconut milk instead of the wheat flour and diary milk. The batter is poured over one side of the heated mould, squeezed together, and placed over a charcoal fire.

In Holland, the same waffle iron is used for both the flat and rolled wafers, so the traditional irons must be robust enough for it to be able to squeeze a ball of dough flat. I don't think most of the round Kuih Kapit moulds used in Malaysia and Singapore are able to achieve that.

I have come across many Kuih Kapit moulds. There are round ones, square ones, and rectangular ones. The square and rectangular ones, which are mainly from Indonesia, appear to be more robust and more similar to the antique iron waffle irons that I have seen in museums in the Netherlands. The designs on these Indonesian and Dutch vintage moulds also look similar.

There are a number of things to prepare before you make Kuih Kapit. These are:

- *Kuih Kapit moulds*
- *A charcoal satay grill if you opt to cook over charcoal*
- *A blunt knife for scrapping off excess wafer from the mould*

- *A ladle*
- *A container for the batter that is large enough to catch the overflow of batter poured onto the mould*
- *An area for scrapping of the excess wafer from the mould*
- *A plate or work surface to fold or roll the Kuih Kapit*
- *A flat saucer to weigh down the Kuih Kapit, if folded*
- *A tube or wooden cylinder of about 2 cm in diameter if the wafer is to be rolled*
- *Air-tight containers to store the Kuih Kapit*

Traditionally, Kuih Kapit is cooked over a charcoal fire. A low fire is needed, hence, start a fire and let it die down to embers before grilling. It is more convenient these days to make smaller quantities of Kuih Kapit using one or two moulds over a low gas fire.

An experienced Nonya or Baba can handle up to eight pairs of moulds with the help of a good assistant whose job is to roll or fold the wafer very quickly before it hardens.

Clean the mould with a tissue and some cooking oil before use, especially the grooves of the design. Then apply a generous amount of oil on both sides of the mould. The first wafer made from each mould should be discarded. After that, no more oil needs to be put on the moulds as there is sufficient oil in the batter from the coconut milk.

There are now a number of brands of electric love letter makers available. They make two Kuih Kapit at a time and are of teflon non-stick surfaces. They even have a indicator light which comes on when the batter is cooked.

Kuih Kapit should be stored in an airtight container in the tropics, otherwise it will go soft in the humid conditions.

Kuih Kapit

MAKES ABOUT 150

250 g rice flour
40 g tapioca flour
10 g flour
6 eggs, approx 60 g each
290 g sugar
250 ml first squeeze
    coconut mik with
    400 ml second squeeze
    coconut milk OR
    250 g store-bought
    concentrated coconut
    milk with 400 ml water

Kuih Kapit molds
A cylinder of 2-cm diameter
    if making rolled Kuih
    Kapit

Sieve the rice flour, the tapioca flour and the flour together.

Beat the eggs in a large bowl and thoroughly mix in the flour mixture and all the other ingredients. Stir until the sugar has dissolved. A food processor could be used. Sieve the batter and pour it into a large container.

Heat up the Kuih Kapit moulds. Open one mould, holding it so that the bottom of the mould is tilted. Scoop a ladle of batter, and pour the batter from the top edge of the mould to completely cover that side of the mould, allowing the excess batter to flow into the container. Any gap will be reduced when the two sides of the mould are pressed together. The batter should sizzle on the mould, otherwise the mould is not hot enough.

Quickly close the mould and replace it over the coals. After about 30-40 seconds, when the excess batter at the edge of the mould is a bit burnt, turn the mould over to grill the other side for another 30-40 seconds. Then take the mould off the fire and use the blunt knife to scrape off the burnt run-off batter around the edge of the mould. Replace the mould over the fire for about 30 seconds

Unclamp the mould to check if the wafer is ready. It should be between light brown and beige. If not, put the mould back over the coals to grill the other side for a bit longer.

When the wafer is ready, use the knife to lift the edge of the wafer from the hot mould close to the hinge of the mould. Then, use your fingers to carefully peel the wafer off the mould. It should come off easily and cleanly.

Quickly fold the wafer into a semi-circle and then fold into two to form a quadrant or into three to form a 60° wedge. The folding must be done quickly before the wafer hardens, so an assistant is needed.

Use a flat plate to weigh down the folded Kuih Kapit to keep it flat.

If the wafer is to be rolled, wrap it loosely round the cylinder and remove the cylinder once the cigar-shape is formed.

Beginners should not use more than two or three moulds at once. The person grilling and removing the wafer must coordinate with the person folding or rolling the Kueh Kapit. Pace yourselves so that no mould will be left on the grill for so long that the wafer is overcooked.

Store the Kueh Kapit in an air-tight container.

Kuih Bahulu   MINI SPONGE CAKES

Kuih Bahulu, Kuih Baulu or Kuih Bolu is made from three main ingredients; my mother's old recipe uses one bowl each of eggs, sugar and wheat flour – but she departed from the norm by adding raisins or sliced bananas to her Kuih Bahulu. This sponge cake is crispy on the outside and soft on the inside. It is traditionally served during Chinese New Year and Malay festivals and ceremonies like weddings and Hari Raya.

The term bahulu, *from* bau dari hulu *meaning 'fragrance from a distance' in Malay, is a very apt name for this cake. Although it is a traditional Malay* kuih, *its origin may be European since wheat flour is native to Europe and not to Southeast Asia. It has been suggested that the name is derived from* bolo *which means 'cake' in Portuguese. The French have Madeleines which are similar, hence Madeleine moulds can be used if Kuih Bahulu moulds are not available. The Chinese also have sponge cakes. There are large ones called Kuih Polu and small ones of different shapes. Katy Biggs, a Facebook friend, has posted several photos of such small cakes taken in Taiwan and also in Kyoto.*

The batter for Kuih Bahulu was traditionally beaten in an earthenware container using a spiral spring wire whisk. It is baked in a brass pan with a brass cover, heated by a charcoal stove from below and embers placed on the top. The pans have from 2-12 individual moulds of various designs.

I asked Auntie Lee Kim Chong and her niece Ang Keng Hoon to give me a masterclass in making Kuih Bahulu. It was organised by Dr Elizabeth Khor who is related to Keng Hoon. On the appointed day, they arrived at my house with all that was needed – the brass pan, a stove, a stool, a bamboo tray, some old newspaper, charcoal, tongs, fire-lighter, a lesong, a hand towel, a lidi, and even a ceramic tile wrapped with aluminium foil to be placed under the hot stove – everything short of the kitchen sink!

Aunty Kim Chong surveyed my kitchen and put the stool next to a wall with the stove in front of the seat. She explained that this was so that one could lean back on the wall to take a rest while baking Kuih Bahulu. All the other utensils were arranged within reach of the stool. The old newspaper was spread on the floor, over which the ceramic tile and charcoal stove were placed. The newspaper was to make it easy to clear up any mess around the stove after the baking was done. Extra charcoal and the tongs were placed to the right of the stove as was the lesong for placing the hot cover of the pan while the moulds were filled with batter. That's why the old-fashion charcoal tongs were needed – to move the cover filled with hot charcoal to and from the pan and the lesong. The tongs were also used to re-arrange the burning coal and add fresh pieces when necessary.

Aunty Kim Chong explained that as we would be filling the moulds with the batter and then using the dirty tongs, she had prepared a damp towel to clean our hands after the operation.

The lidi *would be used to remove each Kuih Bahulu when it is ready. You would prise it off the mould and transfer it to a* karlow *(a bamboo colander) to cool before storage. She was so meticulous, suggesting that the Kuih Bahulu should be sorted out according to colour for a beautiful presentation when they are served.*

With all the equipment laid out, we started the fire so that the coal would become embers when we were ready to bake the Kuih Bahulu. And we were advised to keep the batter away from the fire to prevent ashes from contaminating it.

Controlling the baking temperature by adding or taking out charcoal from the stove and adjusting the ventilating vent is more an art than science! The baking time has also to be optimised to ensure that the Kuih Bahulu reaches its correct shade of golden brown.

My recipe uses an oven instead of a charcoal fire.

During Aunty Kim Chong's masterclass, we beat two batches of eggs – one using an electric mixer and another with a hand whisk – to compare. The results were very different; the hand-beaten eggs were more yellow.

If only one Kuih Bahulu mould is available, divide the egg mixture into three equal portions and make small batches of batter as required. However, if three Kuih Bahulu moulds are available, the batter can be prepared in one batch.

There is now an electric Kuih Bahulu maker in the market.

Kuih Bahulu

MAKES ABOUT 30 USING 18-CM PANS WITH 12 CUPS

130 g flour
2 tbsps cornflour
¼ tsp baking powder
4 eggs
150 g sugar
Vanilla essence
2 tbsps melted butter,
    plus 1 tbsp for brushing
    the mould

Sieve the flour and cornflour, add the baking powder and sieve again. If you are using only one Kuih Bahulu mould, divide the flour mixture into three portions and leave aside.

Beat up the eggs till frothy by hand using a spring whisk. Add the sugar to the beaten eggs. Beat till the sugar has dissolved, the mixture has thickened, and the bubbles disappeared. Mix in the vanilla essence and the melted butter. The traditional recipe does not use butter, but I find the result a tad too dry. Adding butter also makes it easier for the Kuih Bahulu to come off the mould. Divide this mixture into three if only one Kuih Bahulu mould is available.

Heat the oven to 200°C. Preheat the Kuih Bahulu pan in the oven for about 5 minutes. Do not use the cover. The moulds must be hot when the batter is poured in, otherwise the Kuih Bahulu will not come off the mould so easily.

Take one portion of the egg and sugar mixture and fold in one portion of the flour and blend well.

Take out the pan from the oven and brush the individual moulds with melted butter. Do this only for the first baking.

Fill each mould to three quarters full. I use an icing bag because I find it more convenient and less messy.

Place the pan back in the oven and turn the temperature to 190°C to bake for about 8-10 minutes or until the Kuih Bahulu is golden brown. The bottom is likely to be more brown than the top. Prise the Kuih Bahulus off the moulds with a skewer and cool them on a wire rack.

Prepare a new batch of batter when the first has been used. Beat the egg mixture again before combining it with the flour.

Cool the Kuih Bahulu and keep in an air-tight container.

Koay Pai Ti BATTER CUPS WITH VEGETABLE FILLING

Koay Pai Ti, an attractive Nonya hors d'oevre, is made up of crispy shells of deep-fried batter with a filling similar to that of Poh Piah. If the shells are not too big, the whole Pai Ti can be elegantly eaten in a mouthful.

Koay Pai Ti may have originated from Singapore as it was, according to a magazine article published in Penang, also called Singapore Poh Piah. Syonanto Pie is another name, Syonanto being the name of Singapore during the Japanese Occupation. There is an Indonesian dish of Dutch origin known as Java Kwei Patti or Kroket Tjanker, which uses the same Pai Ti shells but filled with minced meat and diced mushrooms cooked in a white sauce. This filling is similar to that of Min Chee, a dish derived from the English Shepherd's Pie. Thus, 'pie' may explain the origin of 'pai' in Pai Ti.

In my mother's Pai Ti, her filling of vegetables, unlike that for Poh Piah which is wet and soggy, is just cooked, drier, and crunchy. There is a practical reason for that; it is to ensure that the Pai Ti shells stay crispy before it is consumed. However, most of the Pai Ti that I have come across, especially in Singapore, uses Poh Piah filling. Thus, the Pai Ti filling of Singapore and Malacca includes taocheo *(soyabean paste) whereas that from Penang does not. Diced, boiled prawns could be used for garnishing Koay Pai Ti, but as Penang food is not ostentatious, this is not commonly seen in the Northern Nonya homes.*

Pai Ti shells these days are, more often than not, store bought, although Pai Ti moulds remain readily available in Penang and Singapore. With very few exceptions, most of the homemade Pai Ti shells I have seen lack quality control. The shape, the thickness, and therefore the texture of the shells, are not consistent, probably because of the lack of experience in making them.

The Pai Ti shell is made by dipping a hot, brass mould in a batter. A layer of the batter forms on the side of the mould which is then immersed in hot oil. The batter is pliable before it cooks, so a variety of shapes for the shell can be obtained by careful manipulation of the mould in the oil. If the mould is moved up and down, a top hat-shaped shell will emerge. The Pai Ti shell will detach itself from the mould when the batter hardens into a crusty cup. If the mould is removed before the batter hardens, the shell would fold up like a clam!

This recipe is based on my mother's original compiled in the 1950s when she gave demonstrations to her fellow YWCA members in Penang. The quantities are sufficient for making about 100 Pai Ti shells. Some of the batter has to be discarded at the end because a minimum amount of batter is required for coating the Pai Ti mould. Therefore, it is best to use a tall cup with a small cross-section to contain the batter for dipping the mould.

Koay Pai Ti

MAKES ABOUT 100

Shells
70 g flour
100 g rice flour
1½ tbsp cornflour
1 egg
1 tsp oil
280 ml water
Pinch of salt
Pinch of pepper

Pinch of slaked lime (*kapur*)
Oil for deep frying

Filling
1.2 kg yambean
   (*bangkwang*, jicama)
200 g bamboo shoots
   (optional)
300 g carrots
300 g French beans
10 stalks spring onions
4 crabs
600 g prawns
600 g belly pork
400 g firm soyabean cake
   (*tau kwa*)
6 tbsps oil
4 cloves garlic
2 tsp salt

Sauce
3 large fresh chillies
60 g peanuts
2 tsp sugar
½ tsp salt
130 ml water
2 tsp vinegar, natural
   vinegar preferred
1 tbsp sesame seeds, toasted

Shells
Sieve the flour, rice flour and tapioca flour together. Beat the egg and mix with the flour mixture. Add the oil and continue stirring. Water should be added gradually as you stir to obtain a consistent thick, liquid paste. If too much water is added at once it becomes difficult to get rid of the lumps that form. The batter becomes thinner as more water is added. Alternatively, the mixture could be mixed altogether in a food processor. Season with salt and pepper and add the slaked lime and stir. Set aside for an hour before making shells.

Heat sufficient oil in a deep pan for deep frying and heat the Pai Ti mould in the oil till the mould is hot. Dip the hot mould in the batter. Do not totally immerse the mould; leave a gap of ½ cm from the top of the mould.

Immerse the batter-coated mould in the hot oil. For a standard-shaped Pai Ti shell, keep the mould steady. For a top hat-shaped shell, move the mould vertically up and down while the batter is flexible. If the vertical motion is excessive the shell will detach from the mould before the shell has hardened, giving rise to a distorted shell. Note that the oil is too hot if the shell blisters.

When the batter has hardened, the shell will detach itself from the mould. If it does not slip off, use a bamboo stick to ease the shell from the mould. Remove the shell from the oil when it is light brown; remember it will continue browning even after it has been removed from the oil. Allow to drain on kitchen paper. Keep in an airtight container.

NOTE: The behaviour of the batter – whether the shell comes off easily from the mould or whether you can make the hat-shaped shell, depends very much on the flour used and the temperature of the oil (about 200°C). In general, the first few shells tend to stick to the mould.

Filling
Reduce yambean by 200 g if bamboo shoots are used.

Cut the yambean and carrots into fine sticks about 2–3 cm long, or shred using a mandoline. Slice the French beans thinly on the slant. Chop up the spring onions and set aside for garnishing.

Steam the crabs and separate the flesh from the shells.

Peel the prawns, devein and dice; keep the prawn heads and shells aside for the stock.

Put the prawn shells and heads with the belly pork in a pot and add enough water to cover the mixture. Bring to a boil, lower the fire and simmer for about 15 minutes. The pork should not be overcooked. It is ready once the meat turns greyish. Remove the belly pork. Discard the prawn shells and heads. Keep the stock for use later.

Remove the skin from the belly pork and the excess fat also if the belly pork is too fatty. Cut the pork thinly into 2 mm slices. Then cut across the slices to obtain strips of about 2 mm thick.

Slice the soyabean cake into pieces of about 2 mm thickness and then cut into 2 mm-strips. Heat the frying pan till hot then add the 6 tbsp of oil and fry the strips of soyabean cake until they turn light brown. Drain and keep aside.

Skin the garlic and chop them up finely. Reheat the oil used for frying the soyabean cake. When the oil is hot, fry the chopped garlic till they are nearly brown. Add the diced prawns and the salt and fry till the prawns are cooked. Include the pork strips and fry till some lard comes off the pork.

Now put in the carrots and fry for 2 minutes. Add the yambean and fry for a further 3 minutes. Include the beans toward the end of the cooking time and fry till it changes from light to dark green. Finally, add the fried soyabean cake and stir thoroughly.

Small amounts of stock can be added during the

frying if the mixture is too dry. If too much stock is added, the mixture will become too wet. The general idea is to fry the vegetables till they are just cooked so that they remain crunchy.

Sauce
Rinse the chillies. Remove the stalks, slit open and discard the seeds. Grind or pound the chillies finely. Pound the peanuts finely.

Mix the ground chillies, peanuts, sugar, and salt with the water. Add vinegar to taste. Sprinkle on the toasted sesame seeds before serving.

Serving
Fill the Pai Ti shells with the filling and top with the crabmeat and chopped spring onions. Serve with the chillie sauce. Fried sliced shallots could also be added as garnishing.

The Pai Ti shells will turn soggy if the Pai Ti is not consumed quickly.

Ban Chien Koay   CRISPY PEANUT PANCAKES

Ban Chien Koay is a sweet pancake which originated from Fujian Province. It is attributed to General Tso Tsung-t'ang, a military statesman of the late Qing Dynasty who suppressed the Taiping Rebellion. He had asked his cooks to prepare a dish that would be easy for his troops to carry into battle, and the result was a folded pancake. This is the same General Tso of General Tso's Chicken, the sour and spicy American-Chinese dish.

Ban Chien Koay is literally slow fried cake – in Hokkien, ban *means 'slow';* chien *means 'fry'. It is made by spreading batter on a round griddle heated over a low fire. When the pancake is nearly cooked, ground peanuts, sesame seeds, and sugar are spread over the pancake. It is then carefully prised off the griddle and folded into a semi-circle and left to cool so that the edge is crispy while the centre remains soft. This is the Ban Chien Koay that I grew up with. Today, sesame seeds are hardly included. Instead, butter or magarine to make the pancake more creamy, and a small amount of tinned sweet corn is added. I understand that in Fukien Province* tau sar *(red bean paste) has also been used as a filling. More recently, other fillings like cheese,* inti *(grated coconut), chocolate and Kaya are offered at some stalls.*

There are two types of Ban Chien Koay – the small, thinner ones made in griddles about 15 cm in diameter and the thicker ones made in large griddles up to 50 cm in diameter. The thick ones are sliced and sold in smaller pieces. The very thin version is crispy throughout.

A similar soft and fluffy pancake called Apong Balek is often confused with Ban Chien Koay. Balek *means 'backwards' or 'upside-down' in Malay, referring to the fact that Apong Balek, like Ban Chien Koay, is folded into a half-moon shape. The reason for the mix-up is probably the similar shape of these two pancakes. The way the Malays, the Chinese and the Indians have adapt each other's dishes in Malaya has also contributed to the confusion.*

The Tamils of southern India have a type of pancake made with fermented rice and coconut called Appam or Appom. It has no filling, other than egg, at least in the version that I grew up with. It is made by pouring batter into a claypot sitting over a charcoal fire; the batter is swirled around in the pot and another claypot filled with charcoal is placed on top to bake the pancake. The non-Tamils, more familiar with the sweet Appom, mispronouced Appom as Apong.

At the same time, the Malays and some of the Nonyas from Malacca and Singapore substituted and added local products like ground rice, coconut milk and/or coconut water, and gula Melaka to the wheat-flour based Ban Chien Koay and called it Apong Balek; some versions do not have any filling but others are filled with fruits like banana, durian and jackfruit.

In Penang, there is a version of Apong Balek much closer to Appom than to Ban Chien Koay. It has grated coconut and has a filling of sliced banana and bits of sweet corn. I have seen recipes with Ban Chien Koay ingredients referred to as Apong Balek; this is misleading. The Apong Balek giddle is similar to that for Apong Bokwa except that the sides of the mould of the former is vertical while the latter is curved.

Ban Chien Koay

MAKES 10 14½-CM PANCAKES

Filling
200 g peanuts
30 g sesame seeds
80 g caster sugar
5 tsps butter
100 g tinned cream style
    sweet corn

Batter
200 g self-raising flour
60 g rice flour
60 g sugar
300 ml water
1 egg
¼ tsp salt
1 tsp vanilla essence
1 tsp lye water (*kee chooi*)
2 tsps oil
½ tsp double-acting baking
    powder

Scrapper to remove
    pancakes from griddle
Insulated gloves
Wooden cover for the
    griddle

Filling
Toast or fry the peanuts till golden brown. When it has cooled down, pound it with a mortar and pestle or grind it in a food processor. The peanuts should be pounded or ground coarsely to the size of fine gravel.

Fry the sesame seeds in a small saucepan on low heat. Shake the pan regularly to ensure that the seeds are not burnt. Immediately remove from the fire when the sesame seeds turn golden; some of the seeds could pop!

Mix the pounded peanuts, sesame seeds and the sugar together and keep aside in an air-tight container.

Melt the butter and keep aside. Open the tin of cream style sweet corn and drain.

Batter
Sieve the flour and rice flour together and combine with the sugar.

Pour water gradually into the flour and sugar mixture. Use a whisk or a food processor to mix till a consisitent batter is obtained.

Beat the egg and combine well with the mixture.

Add in the salt, vanilla essence, the lye water and the oil and mix thoroughly.

Cover the batter or transfer to a covered container and leave to rest for an hour.

Render the double-acting baking powder in 1 tsp of water and mix in well with the batter after it has been allowed to rest.

Cooking

Heat the Ban Chien Koay griddle over a low fire. When hot to the touch, use a paper tissue to coat a thin layer of oil on the bottom and sides of the griddle.

Spread about 4 tablespoons of the batter over the griddle, especially around the edges. The griddle is too hot if the batter sizzles.

Use a ladle to spread the batter all around the side of the griddle. This will give the Ban Chien Koay its characteristic crispy edge. Turn up the heat a little and cover the griddle. When bubbles appear on the batter, sprinkle on the peanut filling uniformly and then drizzle in about ½ teaspoon of butter. Finally, add a teaspoon of the tinned cream style sweet corn.

When the edge is light brown, use a scrapper to separate the crispy edge from the griddle. Prise up one half of the bottom of the pancake and fold over. Remove the Ban Chien Koay from the griddle and place it on a toast stand.

Clean the griddle to remove all the crusty bits stuck to it before making the next Ban Chien Koay.

Repeat until the batter is used up.

Serve while the Ban Chien Koay is still warm and crispy

Apong Balek SOFT BANANA PANCAKES

Apong Balek is a small pancake traditionally cooked using brass moulds. In Malay, balik *means 'return' or 'go back', referring to the folding over of each pancake, hence the name Apong Balek.*

The Penang version has a filling of cream style sweet corn and slices of banana — preferably Pisang Raja, the king of bananas. Grated coconut is added to give this Apong Balek its special bite.

In the main, the version from Singapore and Malacca uses pre-dominantly wheat flour rather than rice flour, but includes coconut milk. It was most probably modified from the Chinese Ban Chian Koay rather than from the southern Indian Appom.

Toddy (or tuak *in Malay) was the rising agent for Apong Balek in the past. Since it is not so readily available these days, it is convenient to use fast-acting yeast instead.*

There are two stalls that I know of which use brass moulds that can make nine Apong Balek in one batch. They are parked outside Union School along Burmah Road in Penang. I understand that they are run by two rival brothers who do not seem to talk to one another. There are some stalls, like the one at Pulau Tikus Market, that make Apong Balek individually using small Ban Chian Koay griddles. An Apong Bokwa pan can be also used. Otherwise, a 12-cm, one-egg non-stick pan will do the job.

Like making Ban Chian Koay and Appom, getting the right temperature for the pan is key. If your stove it too hot even on the low setting, you may have to turn it off for a while. A cover, preferably a wooden one which minimises condensation, is essential.

Apong Balek

MAKES 12

50 g rice flour
4 tsp glutinous rice flour
1 tbsp cornflour
30 g sugar
¼ tsp fast-acting yeast
100 ml water
100 ml coconut milk
1 egg
50 g grated coconut
3 small bananas
Small tin of cream style
   sweet corn
Oil
Paper tissue for wiping pan

Mix the three flours, the sugar and yeast together and gradually add the water and then the coconut milk to obtain a consistent batter. (In colder climates the water and the coconut milk should be warmed up to about 40°C.) Set aside for at least an hour.

Beat up the egg and mix with the batter together with the grated coconut. There should be tiny bubbles in the batter.

Peel the bananas and cut into slices about 3-4 mm thick. Set aside. Open the tin of cream style sweet corn, drain, and it set aside.

Heat up the pan till it is hot. Turn off the heat and wipe the bottom and side with a tissue dipped in oil.

Turn the stove to low heat. Stir the batter and spoon on a sufficient amount to cover the pan to just over ¼ cm thick. Cover the pan.

When the colour of the pancake starts to turn from opaque white to a more transparent white, place a few slices of the banana on one half of the pancake, then sprinkle some sweet corn around the banana slices. The temperature is too high if the edge of the pancake browns at this stage. If that happens, turn off the heat for about 30 seconds before covering the pan again.

When the edge of the Apong Balek browns, separate the edge from the pan to check if the bottom is also brown. If so, fold the pancake over to form a semi-circle. Remove the Apong Balek and allow to cool on a wire tray.

Repeat till all the batter has been used up.

Putu Mayam STRING PANCAKES

Putu Mayam or Idiappam is a southern Indian food which is served as a snack or as a staple with curry. The Indonesians have a version called Putu Mayang while it is known by a slightly different name – Putu Mayong – in Penang. The dish is also called String Hoppers.

As the last name suggests, it is a tangle of string-like noodles. In fact, it looks like the thin Chinese bee hoon *or rice vermicelli. The similarity doesn't end there. I have an old wooden Putu Mayam press that looks like a smaller version of the press used to make the thicker* bee hoon *for Laksa. Known as* sevanazhi *in Tamil, the Putu Mayam press has inter-changeable perforated templates for making noodles and* muruku *of different styles and thicknesses. Choose a template with fine holes for Putu Mayam. A potato ricer could be used as an alternative although the holes are a bit larger.*

For Putu Mayam, it is the practice for the flour to be either steamed, roasted or dry-fried before it is mixed with hot water and salt to prepare the dough. Pandan leaves are sometime added to the flour to give flavour and a green tinge. The dough is passed through the press while moving it in small circles over a bamboo karlow *(tray) to form Putu Mayams. When the tray is full, it is put in a large wok and steamed.*

In Penang, you can find a stall offering Putu Mayam at the Pulau Tikus Market in the morning and in night markets (pasar malam). There is another stall in Pulau Tikus which sells Putu Mayam and Putu Piring at night. In Malacca it is more commonly sold by the Malays.

You don't have to go to the Little India district of Singapore in Serangoon Road to find Putu Mayam. I have noticed several non-Tamil stalls in hawker centres around Singapore selling the dish. Most of the Putu Mayam are factory made in Malaysia and distributed to the stallholders in Singapore.

As a snack, Putu Mayam is served with grated coconut and different types of sugar. I remember brown sugar being used in my younger days in Penang. I have also seen it being served with an orange-coloured sugar, and I must say it goes very well with grated gula Melaka. *The Indonesian Putu Mayang, which is thicker than the Indian and Malayan versions, is coloured red, green and white, and served with a sweet coconut sauce.*

Putu Mayam

MAKES 20

4 pandan leaves, cut into
  2-cm lengths
200 g ground rice
2 tbsps tapioca flour
½ tsp salt
500 ml boiling water

200 g grated coconut
75 g brown sugar or grated
  gula Melaka

Two bamboo trays, big
  enough to sit two-thirds
  way up your wok
Putu Mayam press OR
  a fine potat ricer

Wash the pandan leaves, dry them, crumple and cut into lengths of about 2 cm.

Line the steaming tray with a muslin or J-cloth and sieve the dry rice flour uniformly over it. Steam for about 45 minutes from cold.

Put the rice flour and tapioca flour in a bowl. Add the pandan leaves and the salt, and pour all the boiling water onto the flour, stirring with a wooden spoon until a dough is formed.

When the dough is cool enough to handle, remove the pandan leaves and knead the dough.

Sit a bamboo tray in a wok. Pour in sufficient water to bring the water level to at least 5 cm from the tray. This is for steaming the Putu Mayam.

Remove the tray from the wok and wipe or spray some oil on the bamboo tray. Bring the water in the wok to a boil.

Meanwhile, fill the Putu Mayam press with the dough. Press out the strings of dough onto the oiled bamboo tray while moving the press in small circles to form Putu Mayam of about 12 cm in diameter.

Rest the tray of Putu Mayam in the wok and steam for about 5-7 minutes, or till the Putu Mayam has turned from whitish to shiny white. Remove the tray from the wok and let it cool for about a minute to congeal before transferring it to a plate. If left for too long it will stick to the tray.

While the Putu Mayam is steaming, oil the second tray and press out more Putu Mayam, refilling the dough when necessary.

Repeat with the remaining dough.

Putu Mayam may be eaten with sugar and grated coconut or served as a staple with curry.

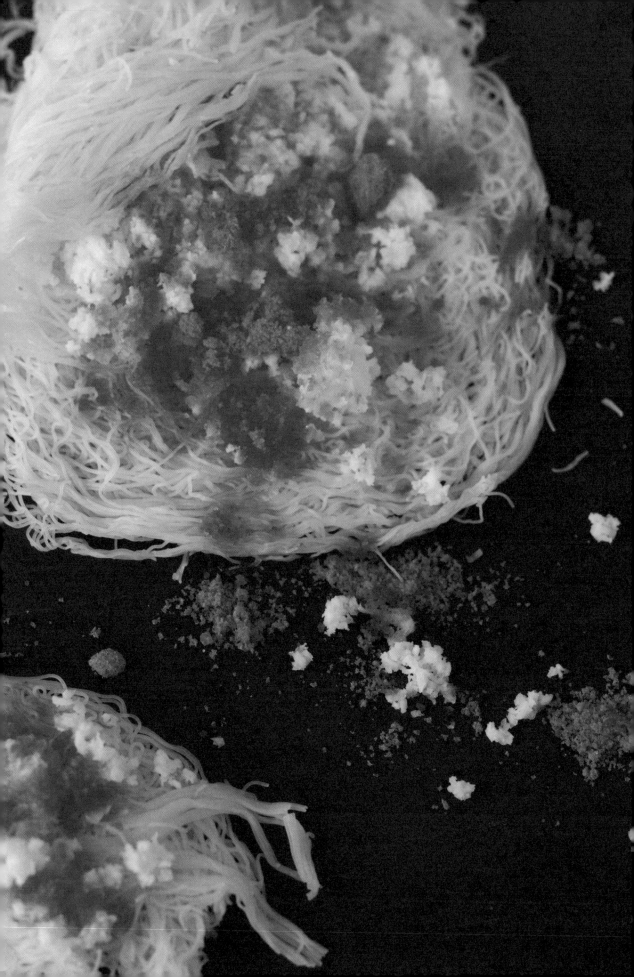

Food Carriers and Containers

In the days before plastic bags, take-away food was wrapped in leaves and newspaper, or we brought our own tiffin carriers to take hawker food home. For formal occasions like birthdays and weddings, the *siah nah* or *bakul sia* was used to carry gifts of food around.

In this section, we also look at the earthernware vessels used for storing rice and water.

Uwa Chan, Mangkok Tingkat or Tiffin Carrier

Multi-tiered tiffin carriers were commonly used in Penang, Malacca and Singapore in colonial times by the Babas to carry food to work for lunch. They were also used during Cheng Beng (All Souls Day) to carry the family's filial offering to the graveside.

These tiffin carriers are called *uwa chan* in Hokkien and *mangkok tingkat* in Malay. *Uwa* and *mangkok* mean 'bowl', while *chan* and *tingkat* mean 'steps' or 'tiers'. In India, they are known as *dabba*, widely used to send food to office workers by the *dabbawalla*.

These tiffin carriers come in two to 12 tiers. They are made of aluminium, stainless steel or enamel. The enamel ones come in various pastel colours and are sometimes decorated with floral motifs.

Tiffin carriers are common again as fewer families cook at home and *tingkat* catering services provide meals. This service delivers a set number of dishes per meal, five days a week. The meals are packed in a *tingkat* of course. Each family has two *tingkat*s; as the one with the food is delivered, the other clean, empty one is collected for the next delivery.

Another type of container we used to take away food was an aluminium canister with a handle and a cover. Today, we can find stainless steel ones. Cylindrical and round

TIFFIN CARRIERS WITH TIERS TO KEEP DIFFERENT FOODSTUFF.

covered enamel pots of various colours are still available. They come in different sizes; the very large ones being used by the hawker to hold soup.

Siah Nah or Bakul Siah

In Hokkien, *siah* means 'auspicious', while *nah* means 'basket'. *Bakul* means 'basket' in Baba Malay. S*iah nah* or *bakul siah* are thus baskets used to carry food during auspicious occasions.

For my maternal grandmother's birthday, we used it to deliver the birthday noodles and Mee Koo (steamed tortoise-shaped buns) to relatives and close friends – one tray for the birthday noodles and another for the buns. Traditionally, recipients of the food will return the *siah nah* with two eggs and two bundles of *mee suah*, each bunch of rice vermicelli wrapped with a strip of the red paper – the type that was used to wrap *ang pows*, red packets of cash gifts.

The distribution of Nasi Kunyit and Ang Koo to celebrate a baby's first month was similarly organised using *siah nah*. The *sia nah* was also taken around when parents personally visited relatives and friends to invite them for their child's wedding. The Babas call this *pung thiap*, literally put down the wedding invitation.

Most *sia nah* are round, but there are also elliptical ones which are not so common. They have a number of tiers, ranging from one to four which sits one on top of another, plus a cover and a handle attached to the bottom tier. *Sia nah* are either made of laquered bamboo or woven bamboo.

The lacquered bamboo baskets, used by Hokkien Baba families, are made in Yongchun, in Fujian province where they have been manufactured for over 500 years. They are first woven from bamboo and then lacquered black and red, and gilded with auspicious designs. Some of these baskets have three-dimensional decorations. Black and gold tiered baskets are less common. Another feature of these baskets is that one of the tiers has small holes on the side to allow for ventilation when hot food is carried about.

The bamboo baskets used by the Teochews are not lacquered but they are painted with auspicious motifs such as fruits like pomegranates and flowers like peonies. Some large baskets of this type have a small, loop attached to the top of the handle to allow a pair of baskets to be carried on each end of a pole over the shoulder. There are other bamboo baskets, including hexagonal ones, made in other regions of China.

The Indian hawkers carried their Nonya *kuih*s and Laksa ingredients in Teochew bamboo baskets – one at each end of a pole known as *kandar* in Malay. The pot of Laksa gravy and the stove it sat on was carried hung on the pole between the baskets.

TEOWCHEW–STYLE *SIAH NAH* (FOREGROUND) AND THE HOKKIEN KIND.

"Belling"

Earthenware Vessels

Large earthenware jars made in Chinese or Southeast Asian kilns were used to store large quantities of rice in the Nonya kitchen. A wooden lacquered *dulang* ('tray' in Malay) was traditionally used to cover the jar. I remember placing unripe fruits like chiku and nona (custard apple) in the rice to accelerate the ripening process.

Large earthenware tubs with a dragon motif on the outside and a deep celadon green on the inside were traditionally used in Nonya households to store water in the kitchen or bathroom. There was a very large one in my grandmother's house in Macalister Road. You could have a bath in it.

Hot Water Flask

Hot water in the past was stored in vacuum flasks, some decorated with pretty floral designs. They have cork stoppers lined with muslin and an outer metal cover. The internal structure of the flasks is basically two layers of glass with a vacuum in between to prevent heat loss.

The old hot water flasks broke easily if not carefully handled. Today, we have unbreakable vacuum flasks made of stainless steel instead of glass, and electrical hotpots which provide hot water on-tap.

RESOURCES

New Nonya kitchen utensils are available at the following shops. The items are listed and spelled as they appear in the online stores. Do not include the descriptions within square brackets when using the shops' search function.

ONLINE STORES
http://www.bakingfrenzy.com
Traditional Kuih Pie Tee
  (Top Hat Mini Tart) Shell Mold
Wooden Ang Ku Kueh Mold
Kueh Bangkit Mold
Ban Chang Kuih [mould]
Kue Apam Balik [mould]
Kuih Murukku Putu Mayam Maker Press
Roti Jala [cups]
Norwegian krumkake waffle cookie press
  [Kuih Kapit iron]
Traditional 12 Leaf madeleine muffin tin
  / kuih bahulu mould
Traditional 3 Koi fish madeleine muffin
  tin / kuih bahulu mould
Traditional 7 Flower madeleine muffin tin
  / kuih bahulu mould

http://www.cookingoddities.com
Kueh Pie Tee Molds [Thai style]
Roti Jala cups
Kanom krok / Thai Desert Pan
  [Thai style Kueh Bahulu pan]
Hot pot [Steamboat]

http://www.templeofthai.com
[Listed under Cookware]
Mortar and pestle
Steamers
Woks [brass and carbon steel]
[Cookware: Thai Dessert Cookware]
Pai Tee moulds (Thai style)
Kueh Bahulu pans (Thai style)
Kuih Bangkit mounds (Thai style)
[Cookware: Grills, Hot Pots & Platters]
Thai claypot
Hot pot (Steamboat)
Hot pot brass skimmers (Steamboat nets)
Charcoal oven

[Cookware: Cooking Utensils]
Skimmers
Tiffin carrier
Bamboo skewers

http://mytakada.com
Electric love letter maker
Electric doughcake Toaster [Kuih Bahulu]

https://www.iona.com.sg
Electric love letter maker Model: GL8388

SINGAPORE
5B
46 Joo Chiat Road
Singapore 427368

Ailin Bakery
845 Geylang Road
#01- 48 Tanjong Katong Complex
Singapore 400845

Bake King
Blk 10 Haig Road, #01-363/365
Singapore 430010

Kitchen Capers
Block 71 #01-531F Kallang Bahru
Singapore 330071

Phoon Huat
100 North Buona Vista,
#02-01 Buona Vista MRT Station,
Singapore 139345
(Many other branches)

Sun Lik Trading Pte Ltd
33 Seah Street
Singapore 188389

MALACCA
Cookware shops along Jalan Kg Jawa.

KUALA LUMPUR
Bake with Yen
29 & 33, Lorong Haji Taib Satu 50350
Kuala Lumpur
(Many other branches)

Chang Tung
26, Jalan SS24/13
Taman Megah
47301 Taman Megah
Selangor

Kwong Yik Seng Crockery Sdn Bhd
144 Jalan Tun H S Lee
Kuala Lumpur

PENANG
Demeters Choice Trading
598H Jalan Jelutong
11600 Penang

GA Baker Paradise
26 Jalan Penaga
Jelutong Market
11600 Penang

Pots Kitchenwares Sdn Bhd
49-51 Kuala Kangsar Road
10100 Penang

Sim Company Sdn Bhd
193 & 195, Lebuh Carnavon
10100 Penang

Teow Hin Chan
224 Lebuh Pantai
10300 Penang

Thow Seng Chan Crockery
266-A, Lebuh Carnarvon
10100 Penang

Stall at Pulau Tikus Market near the
Cantonment Road end of market.

INDEX

Pages with recipes are set in bold.

ACKNOWLEDGEMENTS

Publishing a heritage cookbook like this would be unattainable without lots of help from friends and relatives. So many played their part that it is impossible to name every individual.

I am grateful to my mentor, Mdm Lim Say Choo, who taught me all about making *kuih*s. Unfortunately she passed away in 2014.

Special thanks to my wife and my children Kim, Clara, and Mark, and my granddaughter Alice who helped eat the food I cooked in preparing this book.
Alice had her first taste of Koay Pai Ti on her first birthday; it is one of her favourite dishes.

I would also like to thank:
Cousin Sandy Gee who went out of her way to show me how to cook a number of family dishes.

My brothers Jin Eong and Jin Leong, and sisters Jin Inn and Jin Ai for clarifying details about our mother's cooking.

Dr Elizabeh Khor for organizing the Kuih Bahulu masterclass conducted by Aunty Lee Kim Chong and her assistant Ang Keng Hoon.

The many friends and relatives who gave me heritage utensils and old recipe books.

Cousins Chai Kulvanick, and Maureen and Laurence Chan who provided some old photographs.

Cheryll Ng, Pauline Ong, and Clara Ong who helped with proofreading.

Friends from my Penang Heritage Food Facebook group who offered suggestions.